Volume 03

Infinite Colors Saga: Adult Coloring Book Series

Luna Scarlet

ANIME
COLORING BOOK
FOR ADULTS

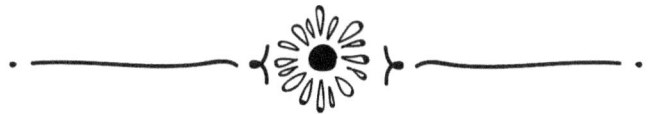

How to Use This Book

Whether you are a seasoned colorist or just beginning, this book is for you. You can use pencils, markers, or even paints – whatever medium brings you the most joy. Don't worry about staying within the lines; this is your personal journey through landscapes. Feel free to experiment with colors and techniques to make each scene your own.

Tips and Techniques

- **Layering and Blending:** Experiment with layering colors and blending them to create depth and texture.
- **Light and Shadow:** Play with light and shadow to bring the landscapes to life.
- **Color Choices:** There are no rules – vibrant, muted, monochrome, or even abstract color schemes can transform each scene.
- **Take Breaks:** Enjoy the process and don't rush. Coloring is a meditative activity; take it one page at a time.

Color Tester

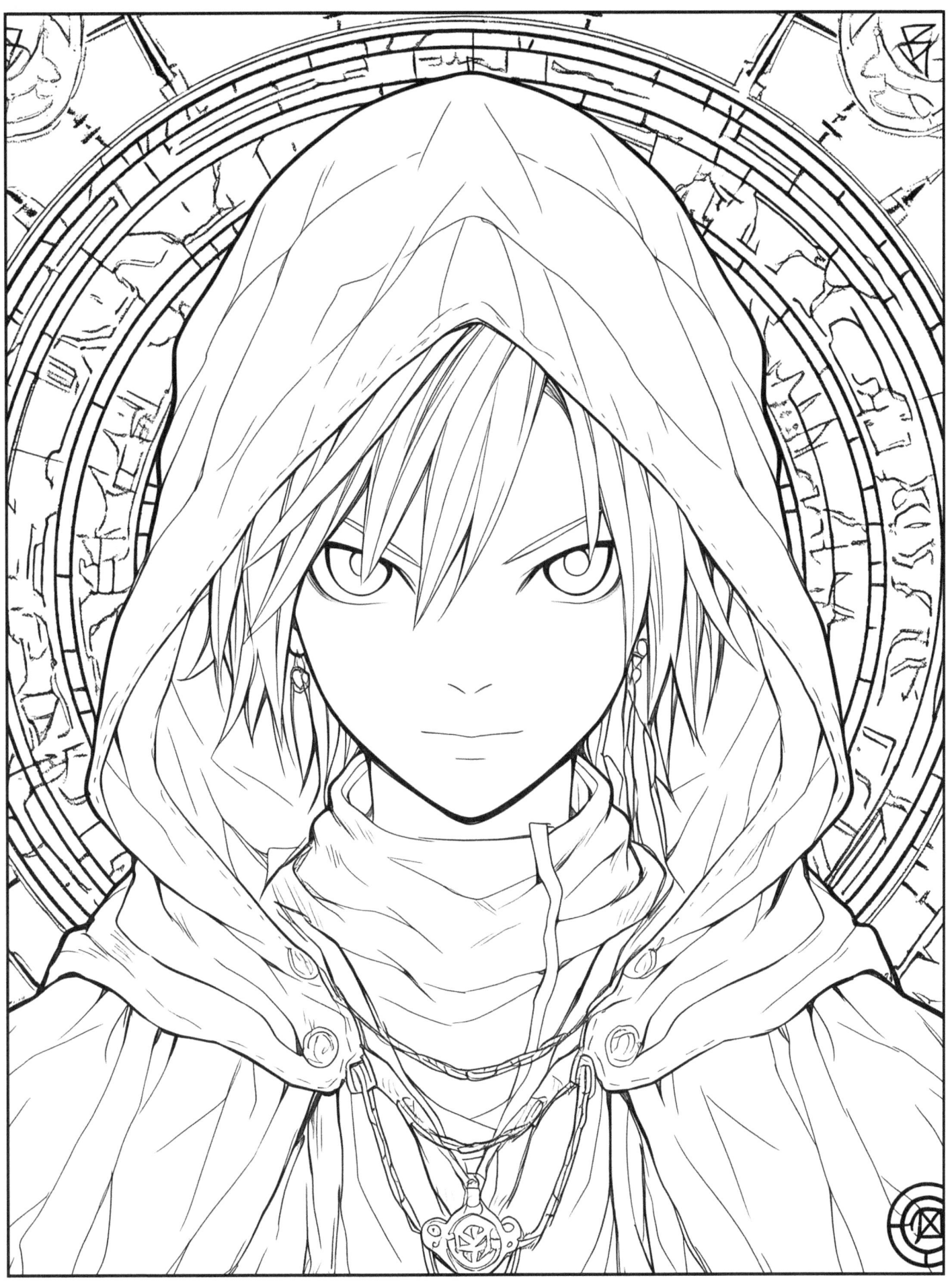

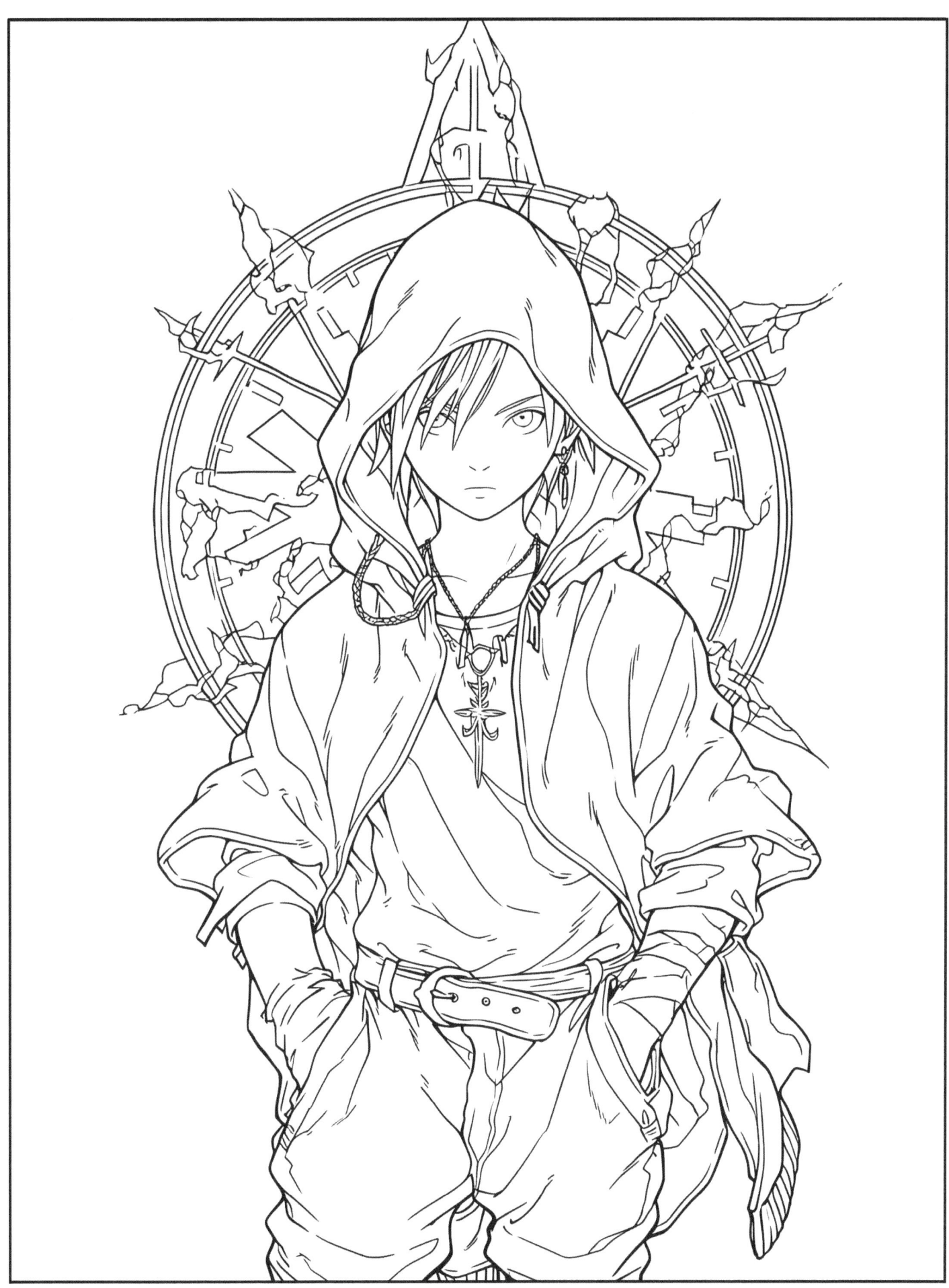

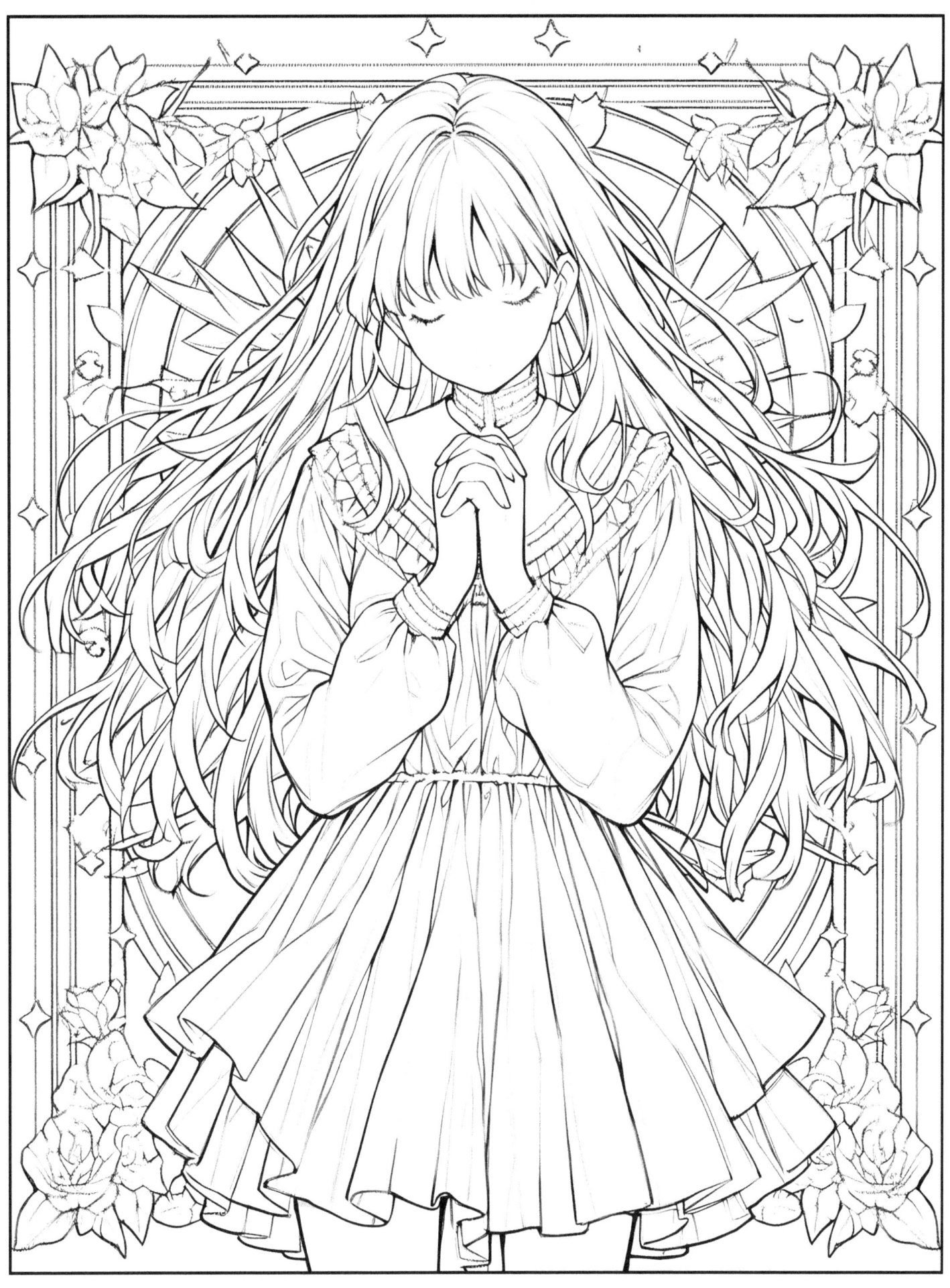

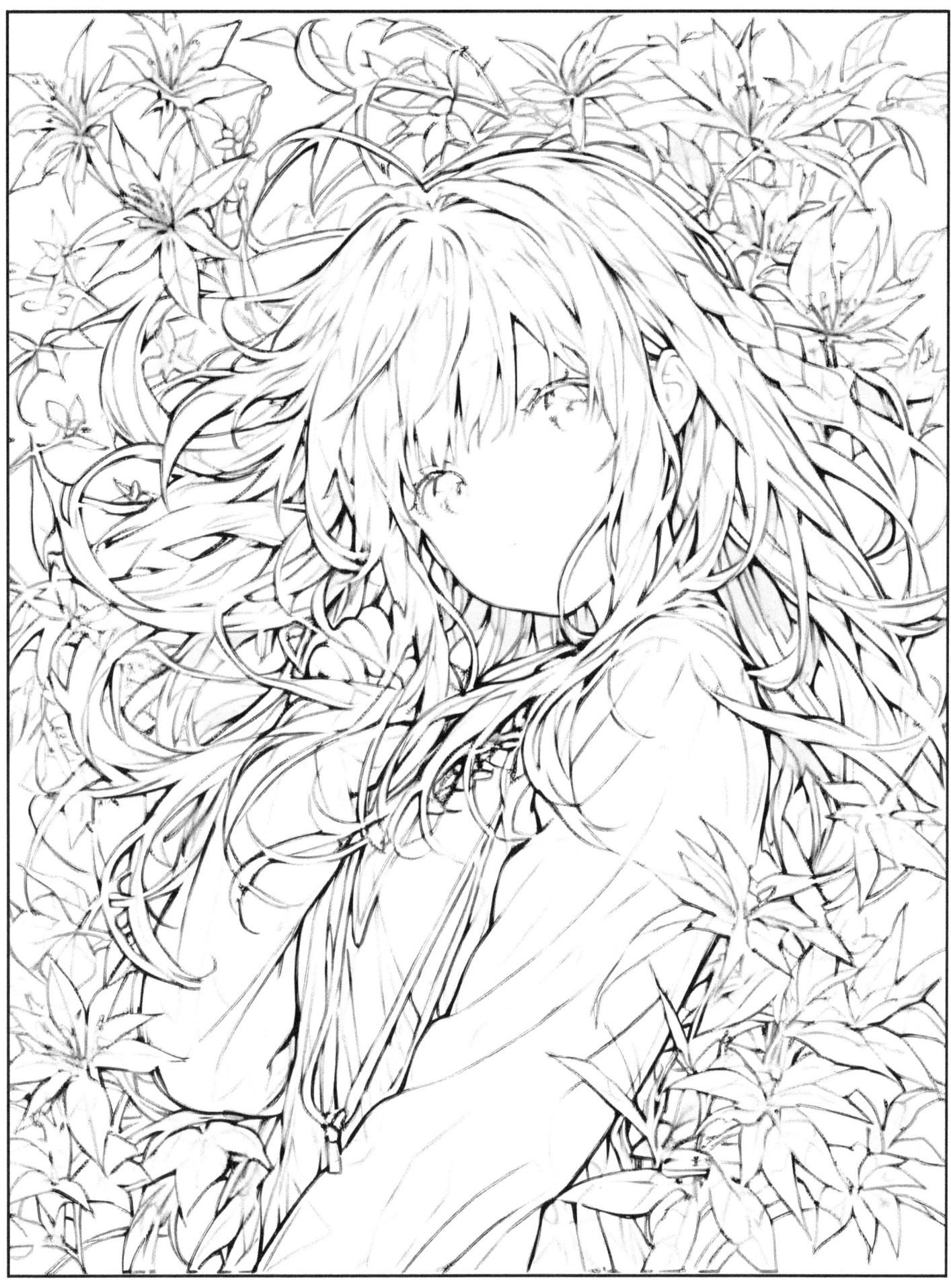

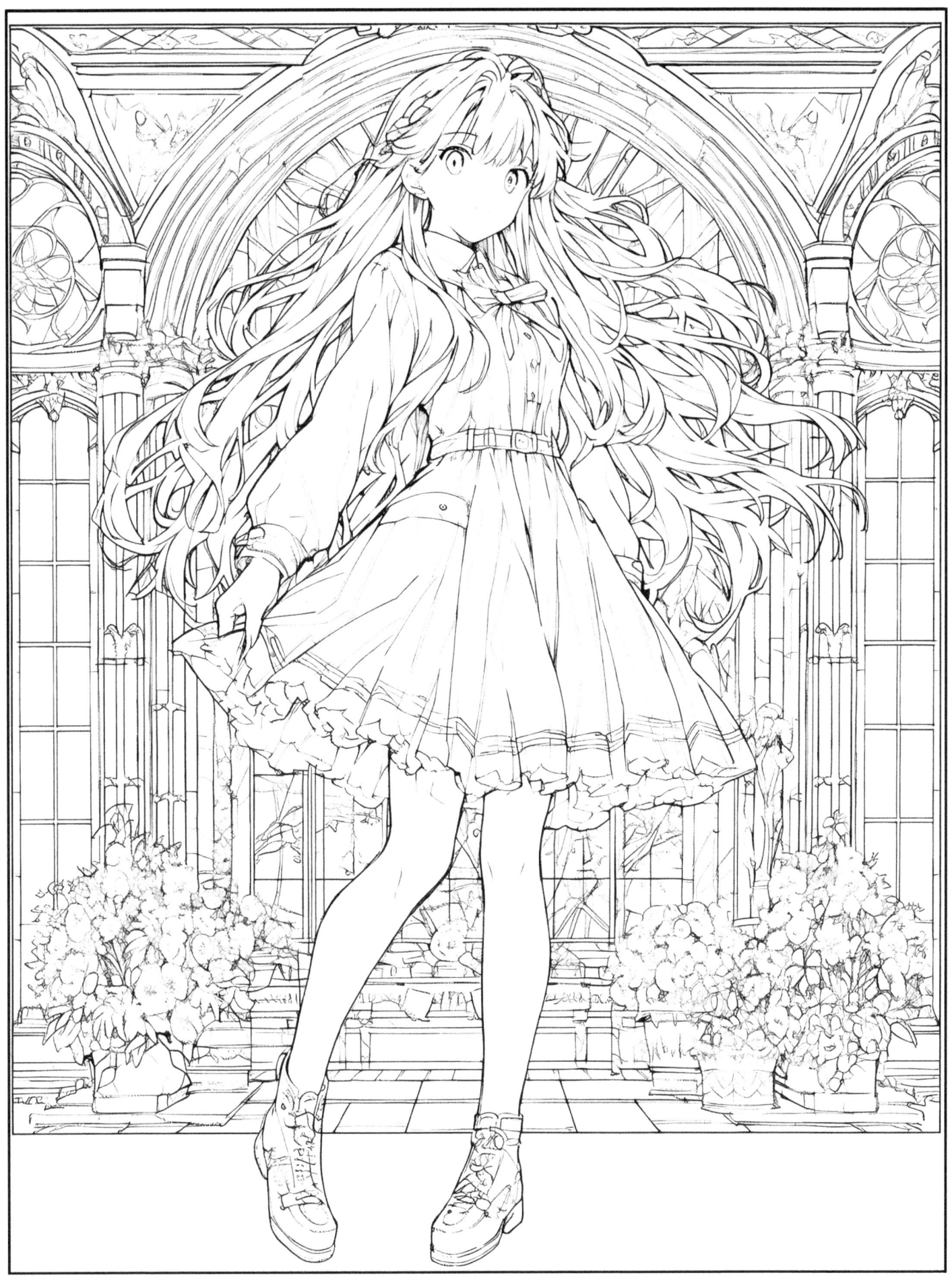

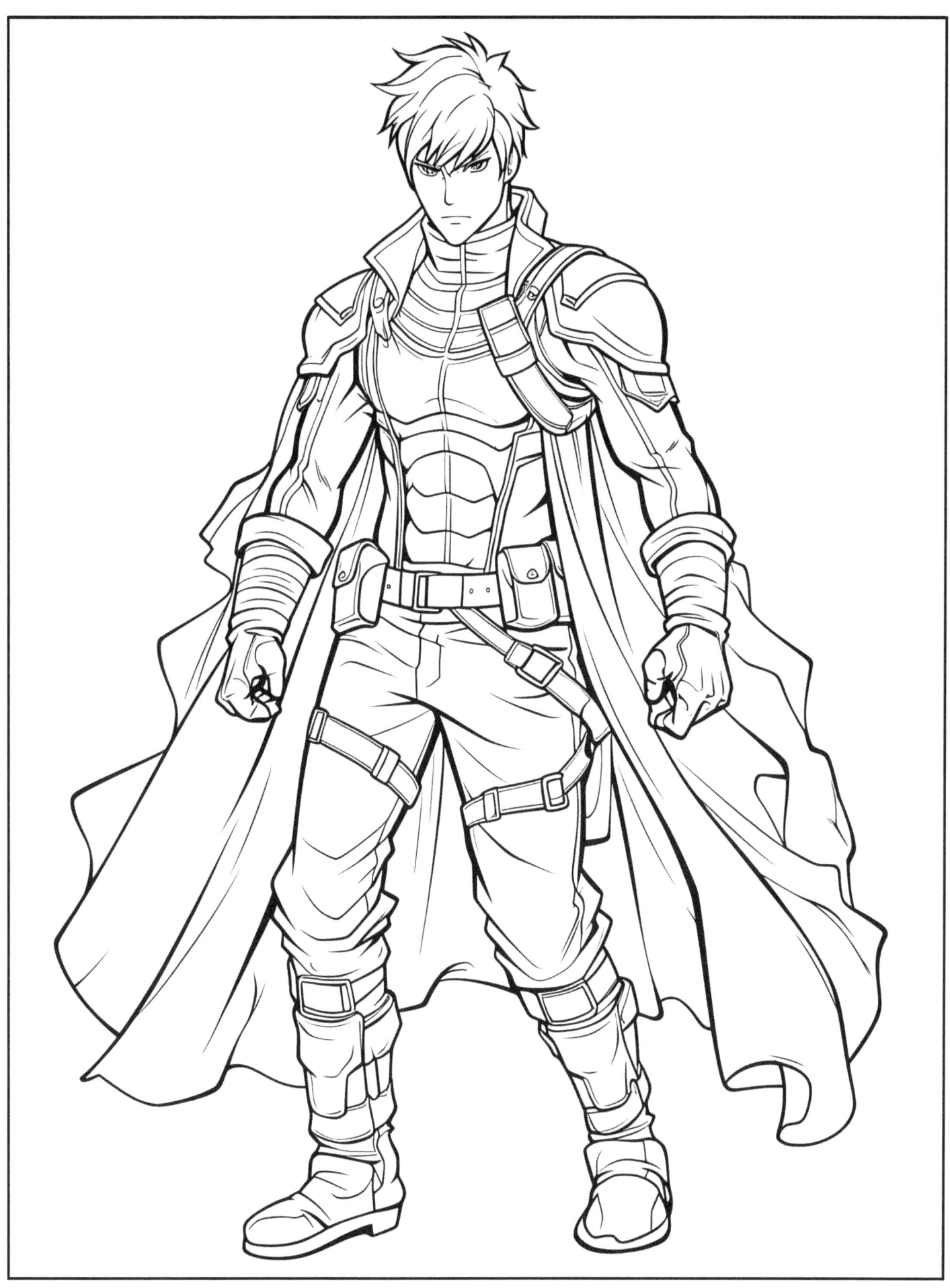

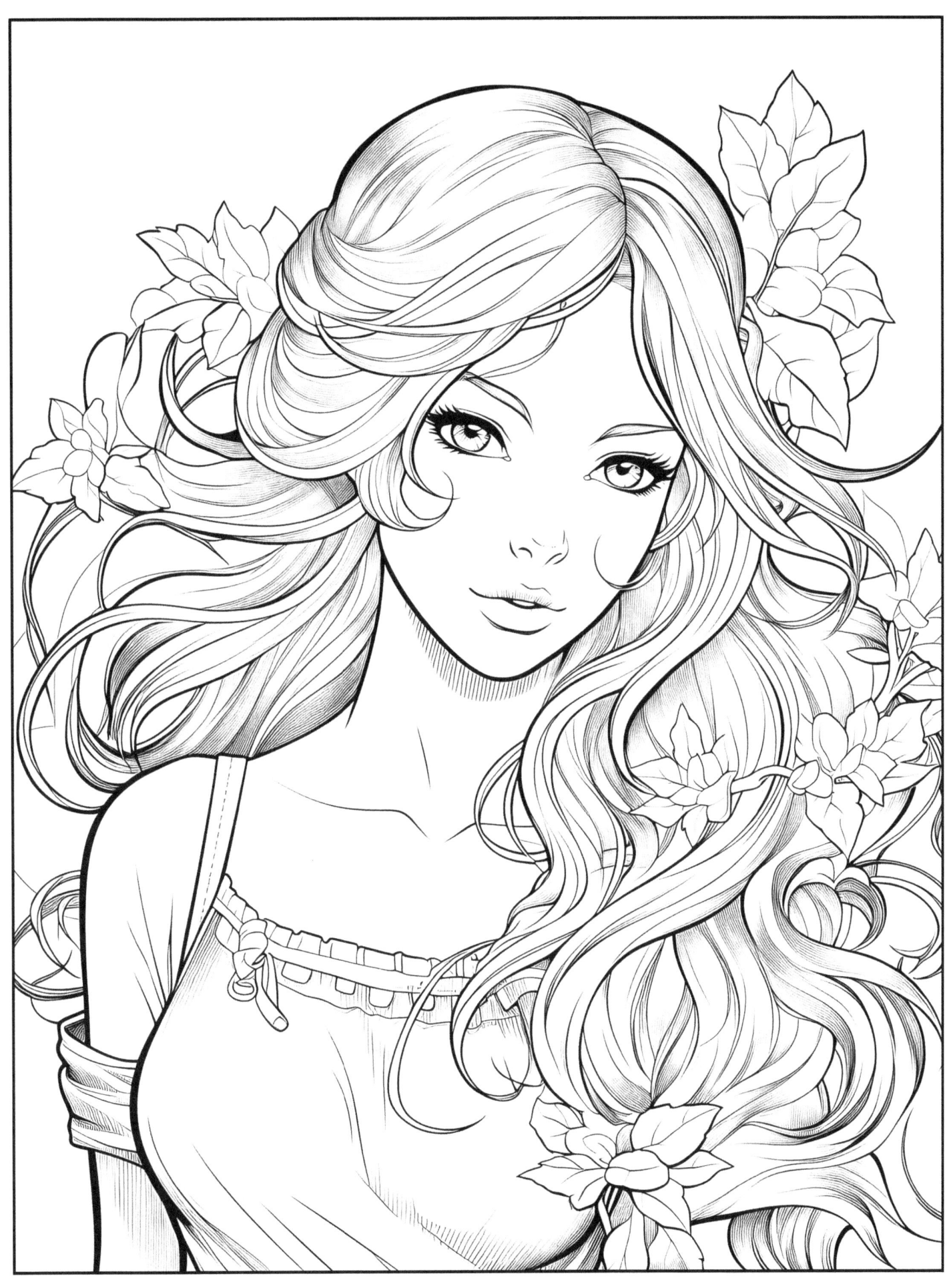

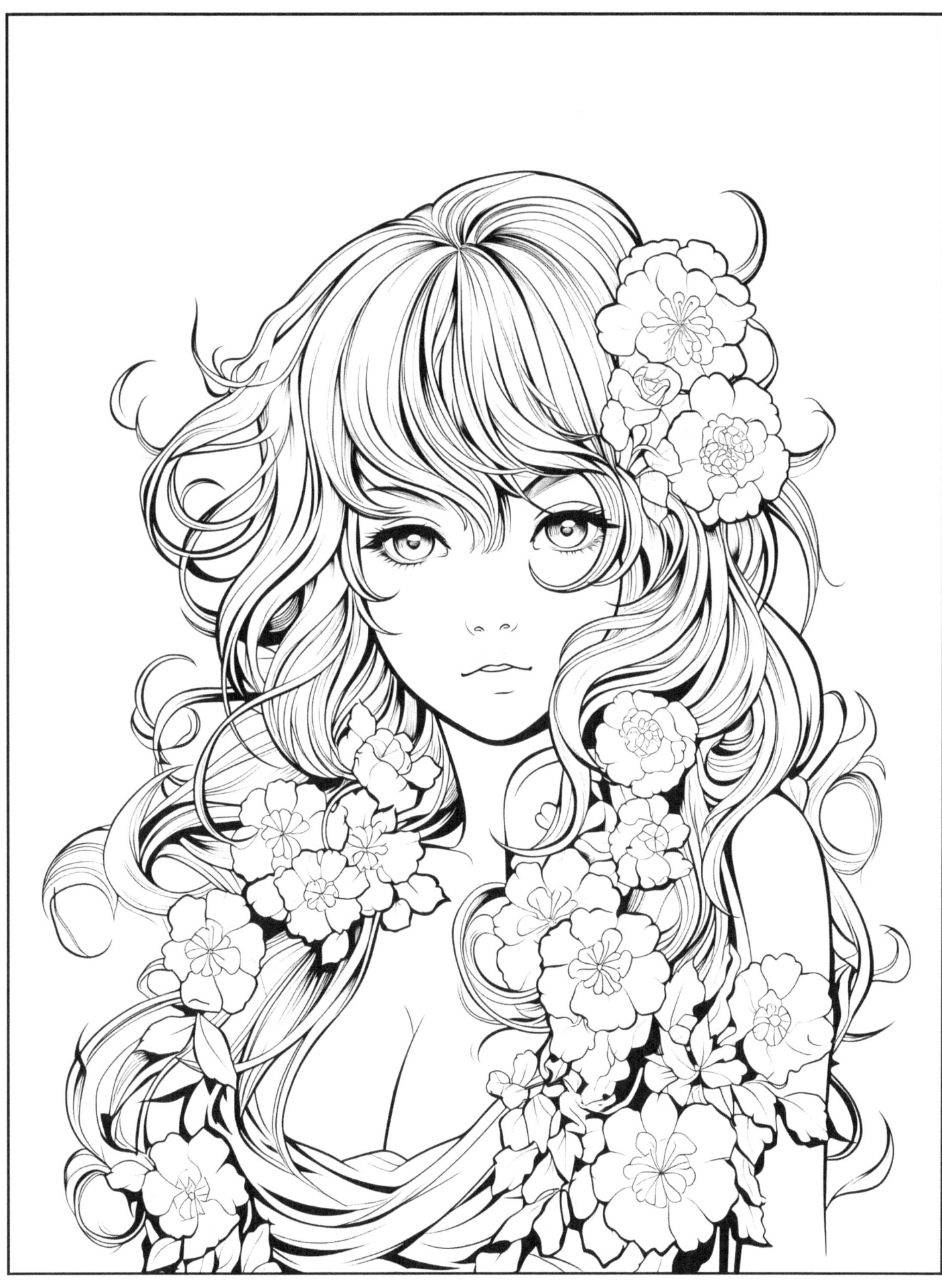

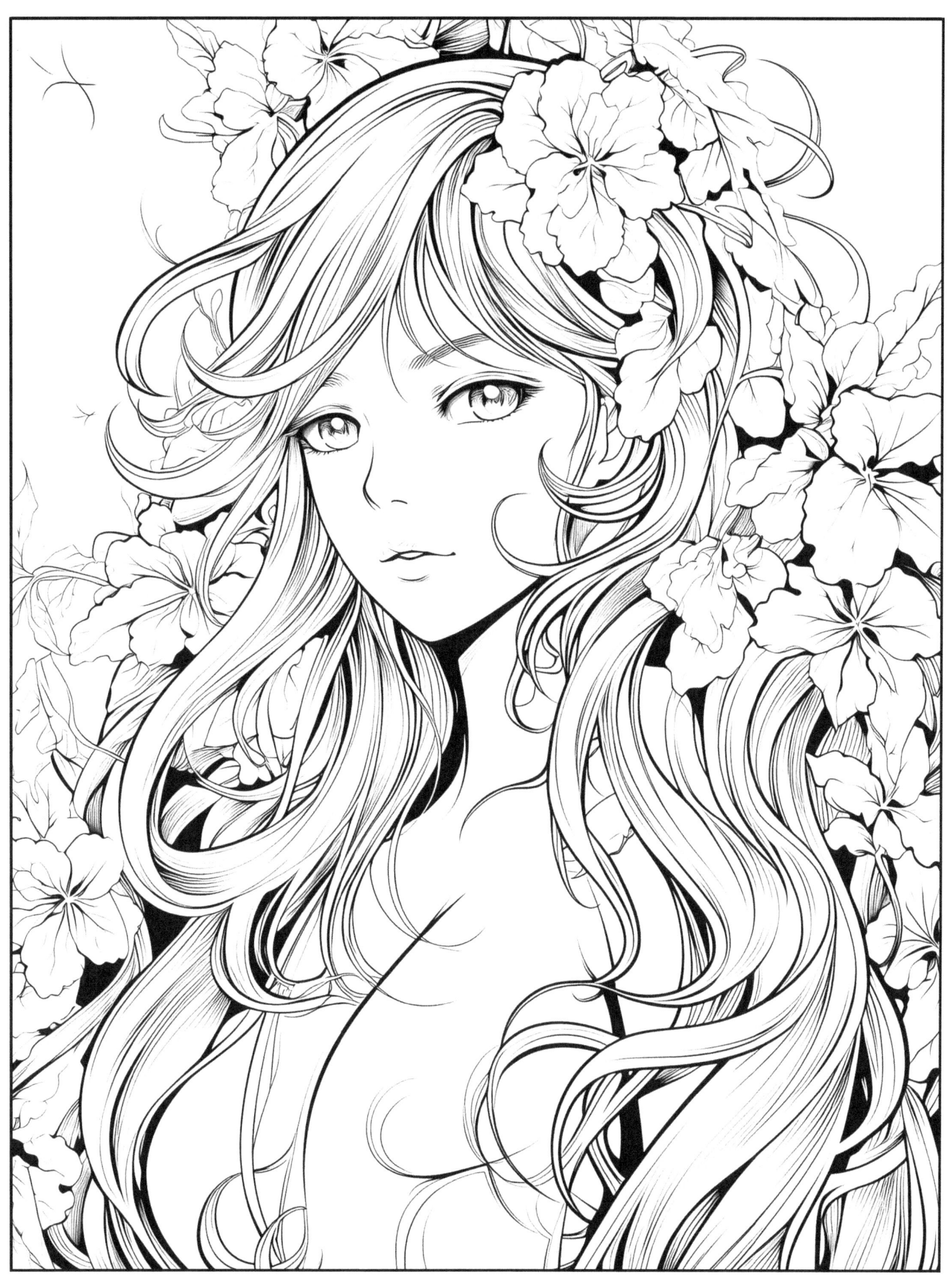

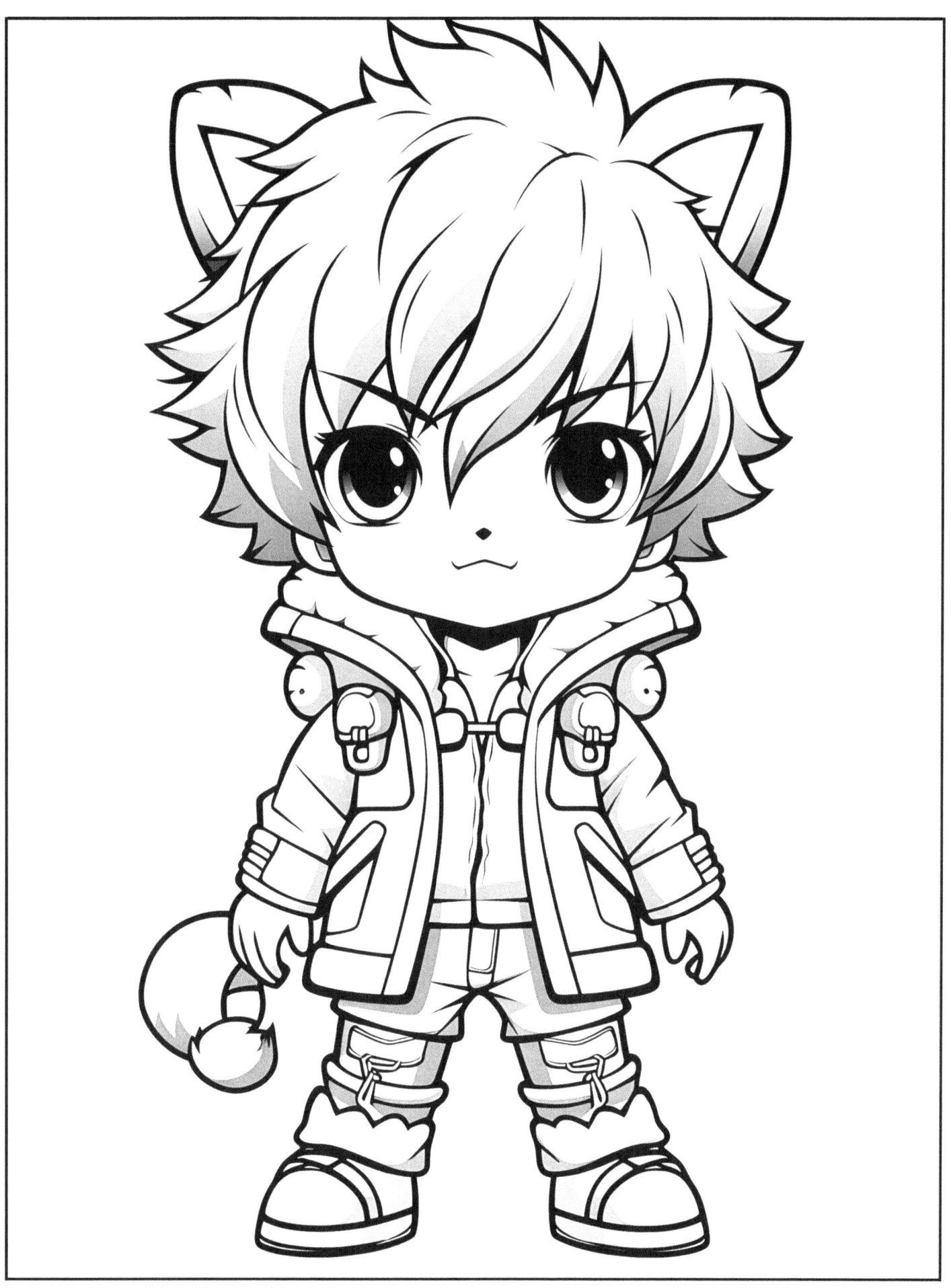

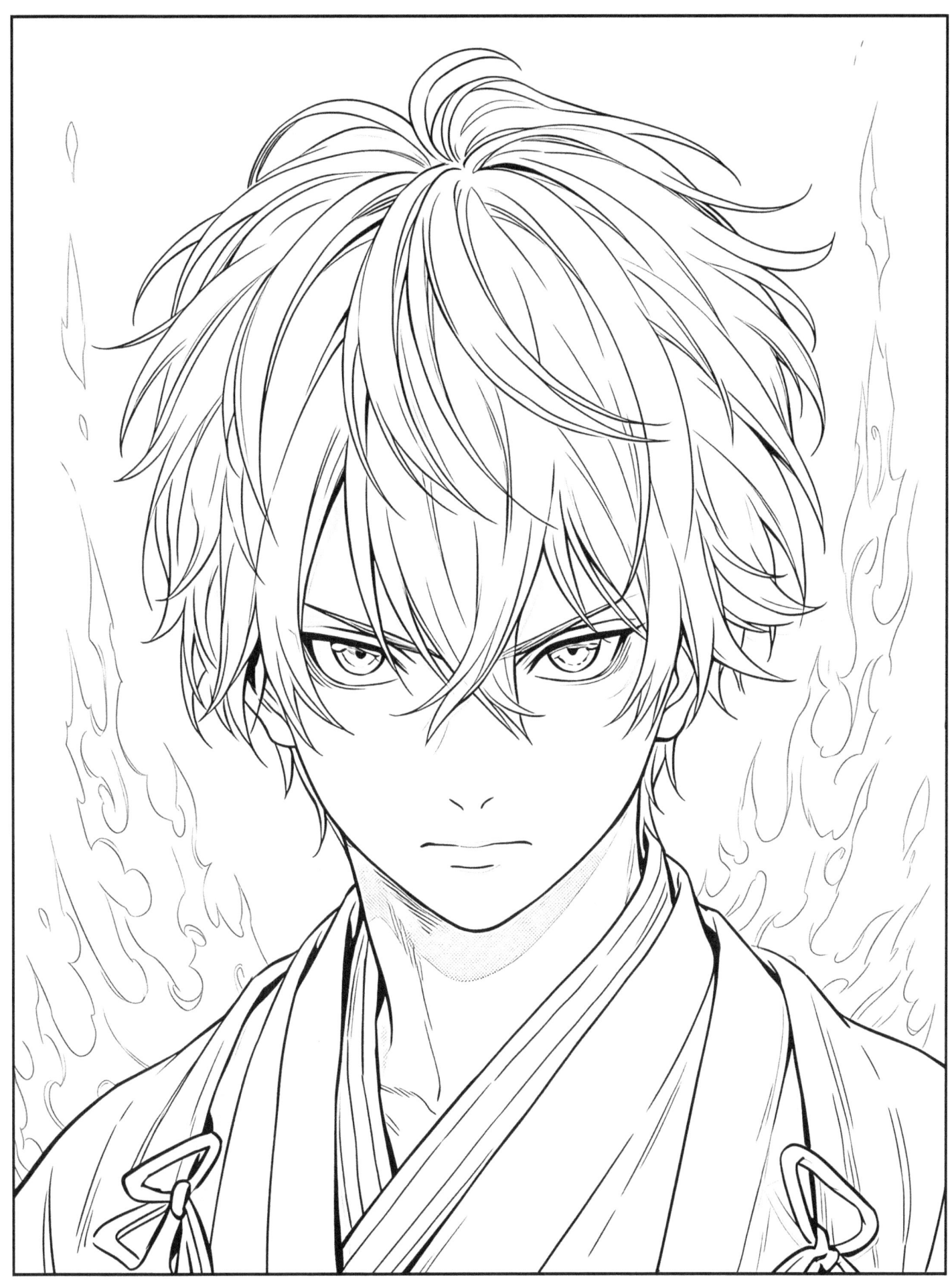

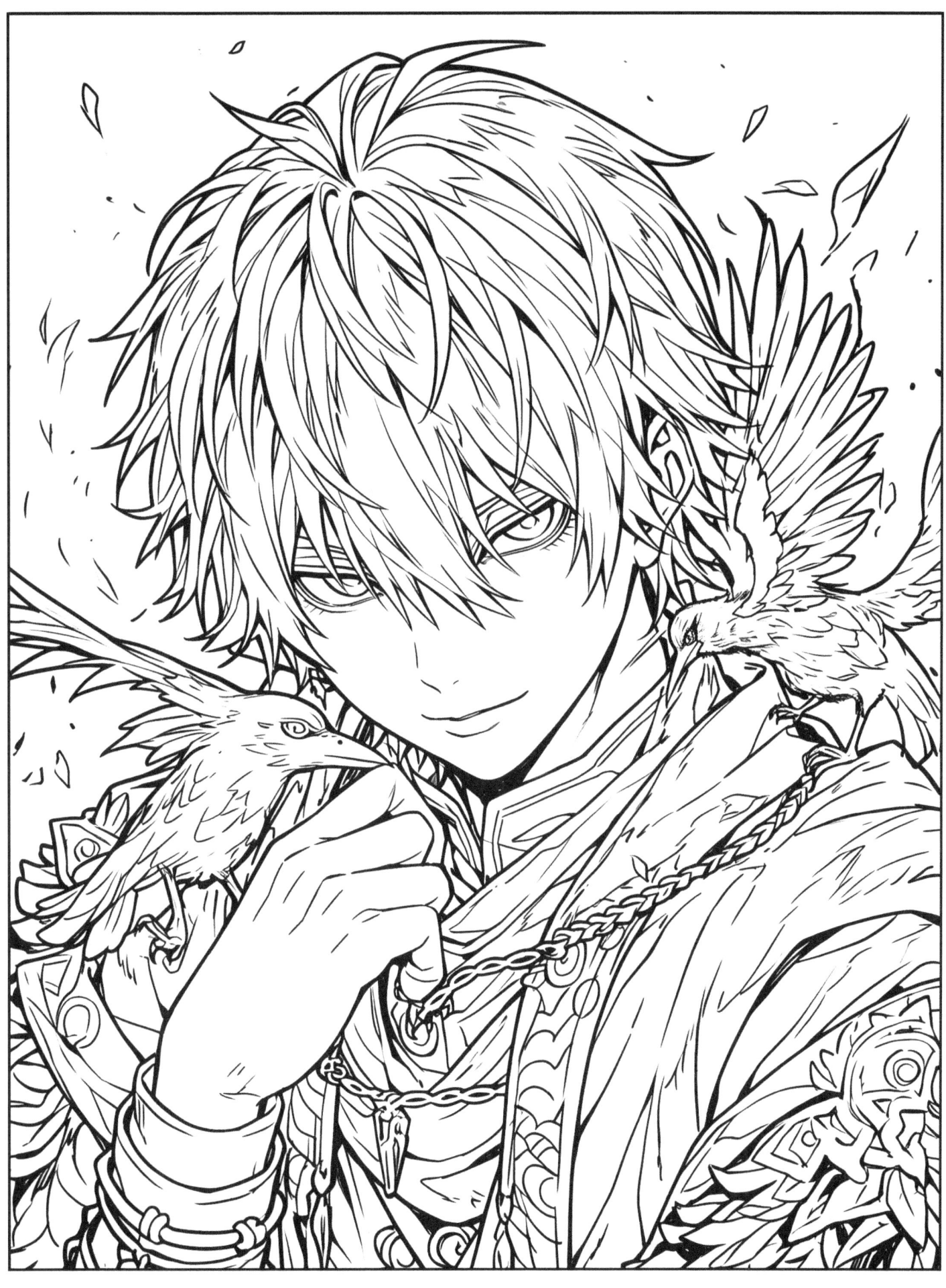

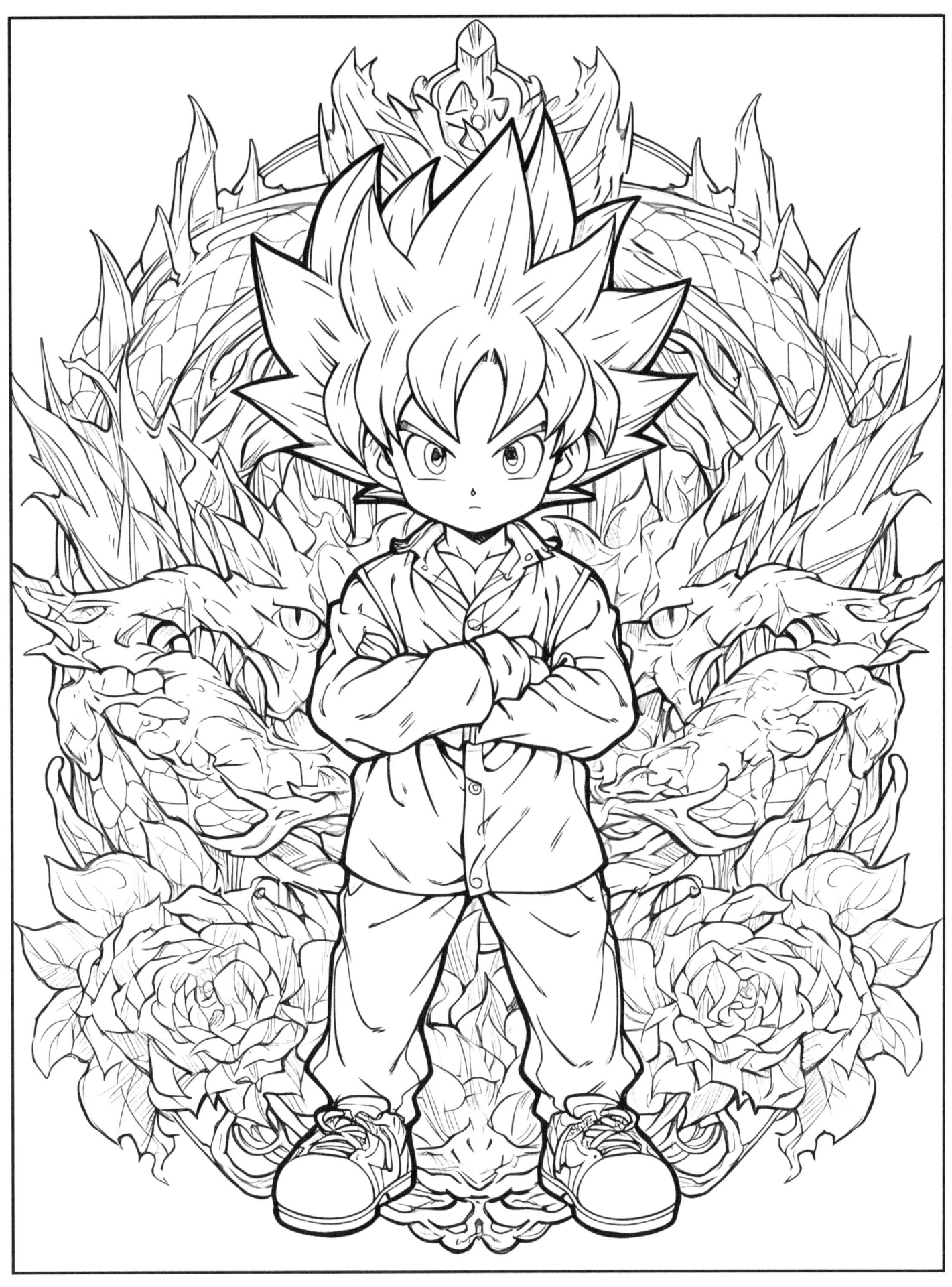

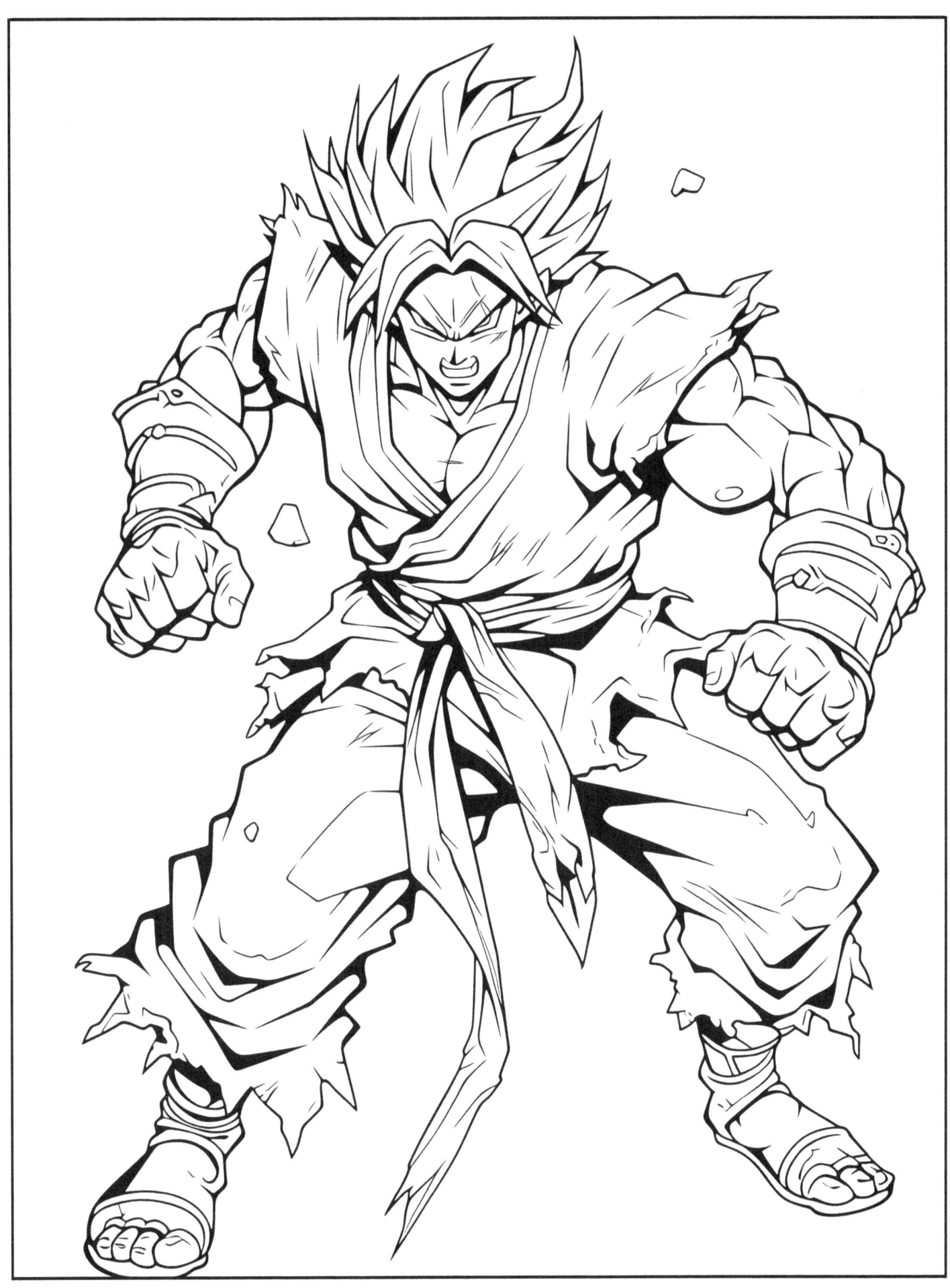

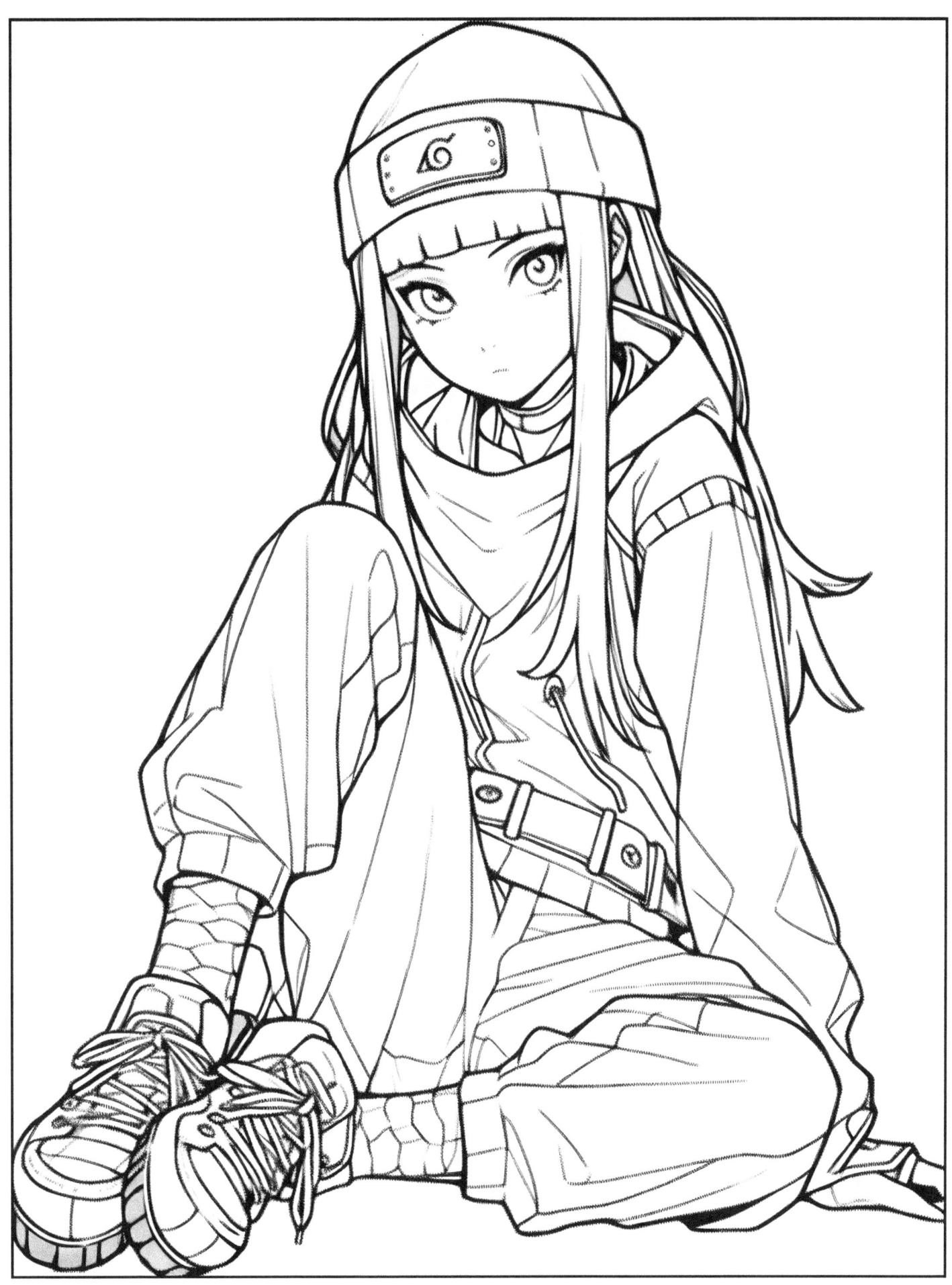

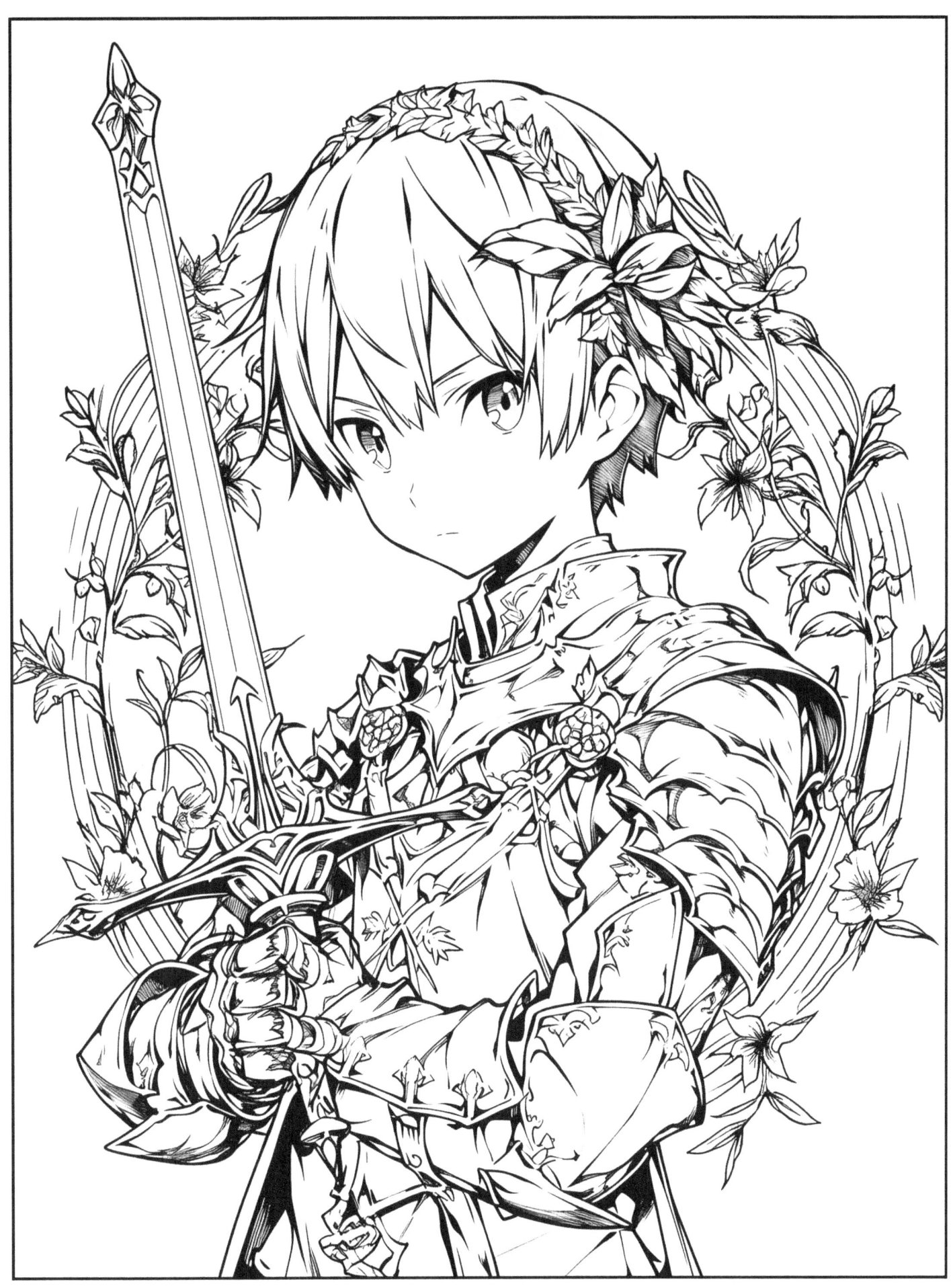

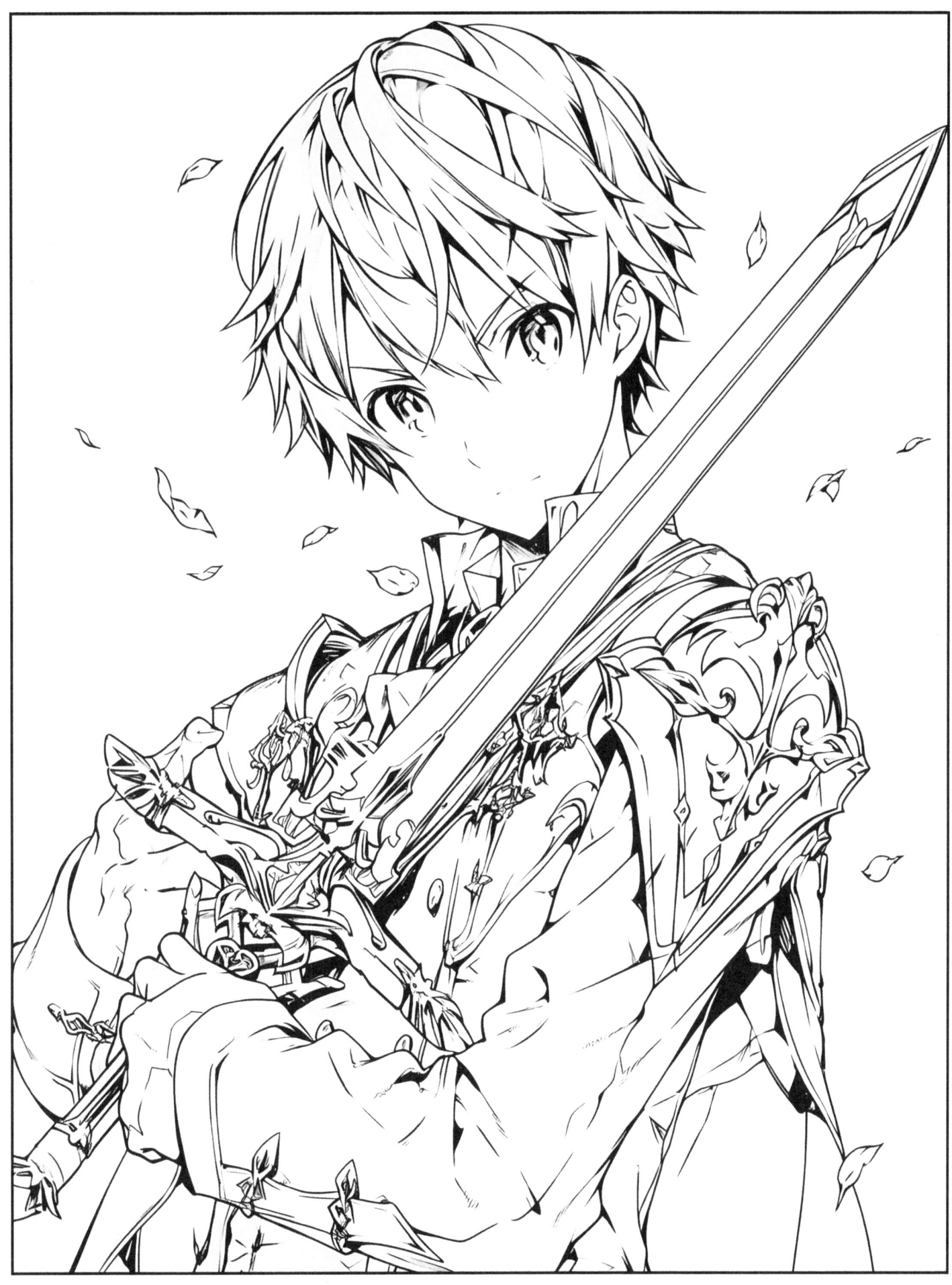

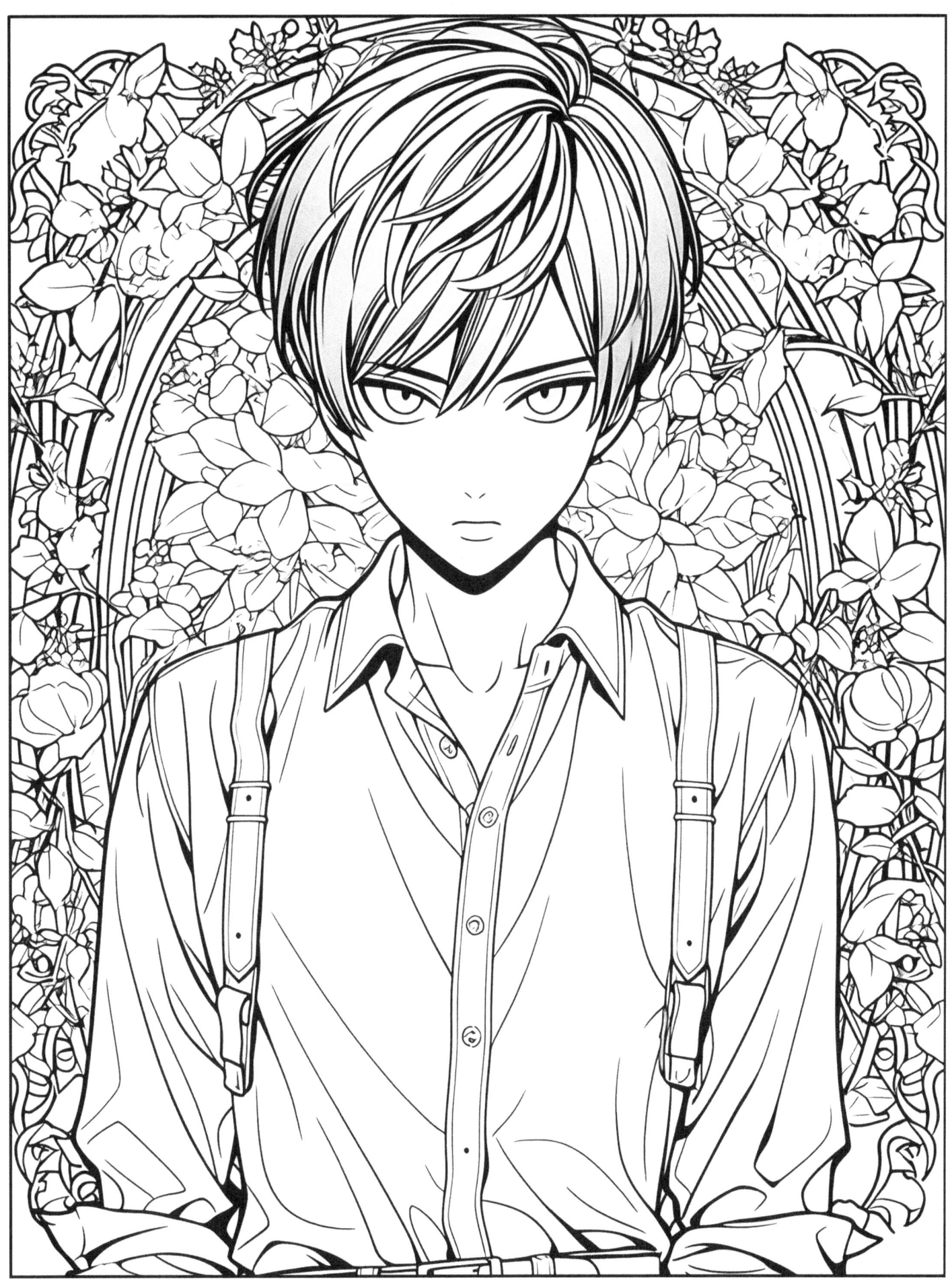

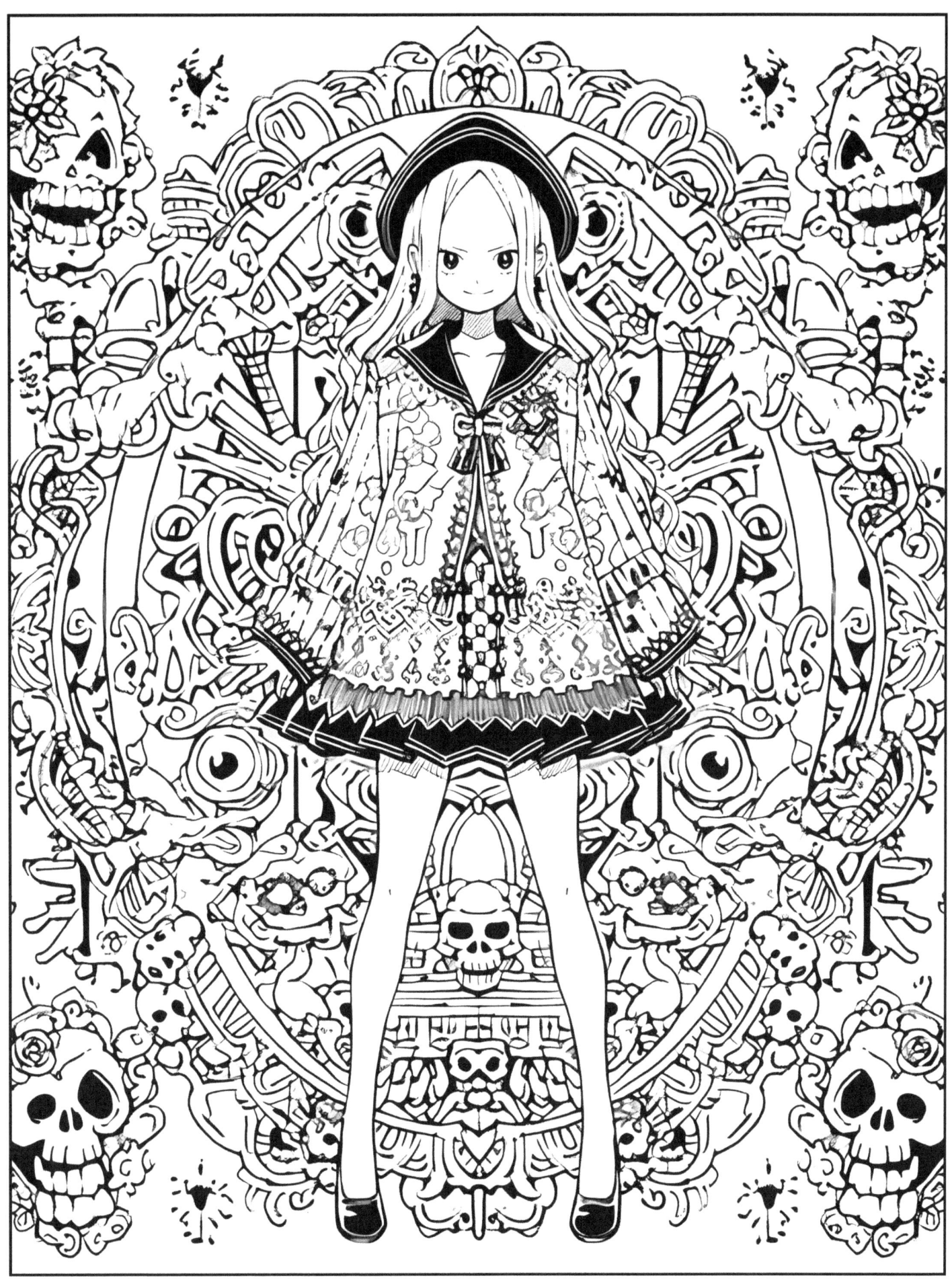

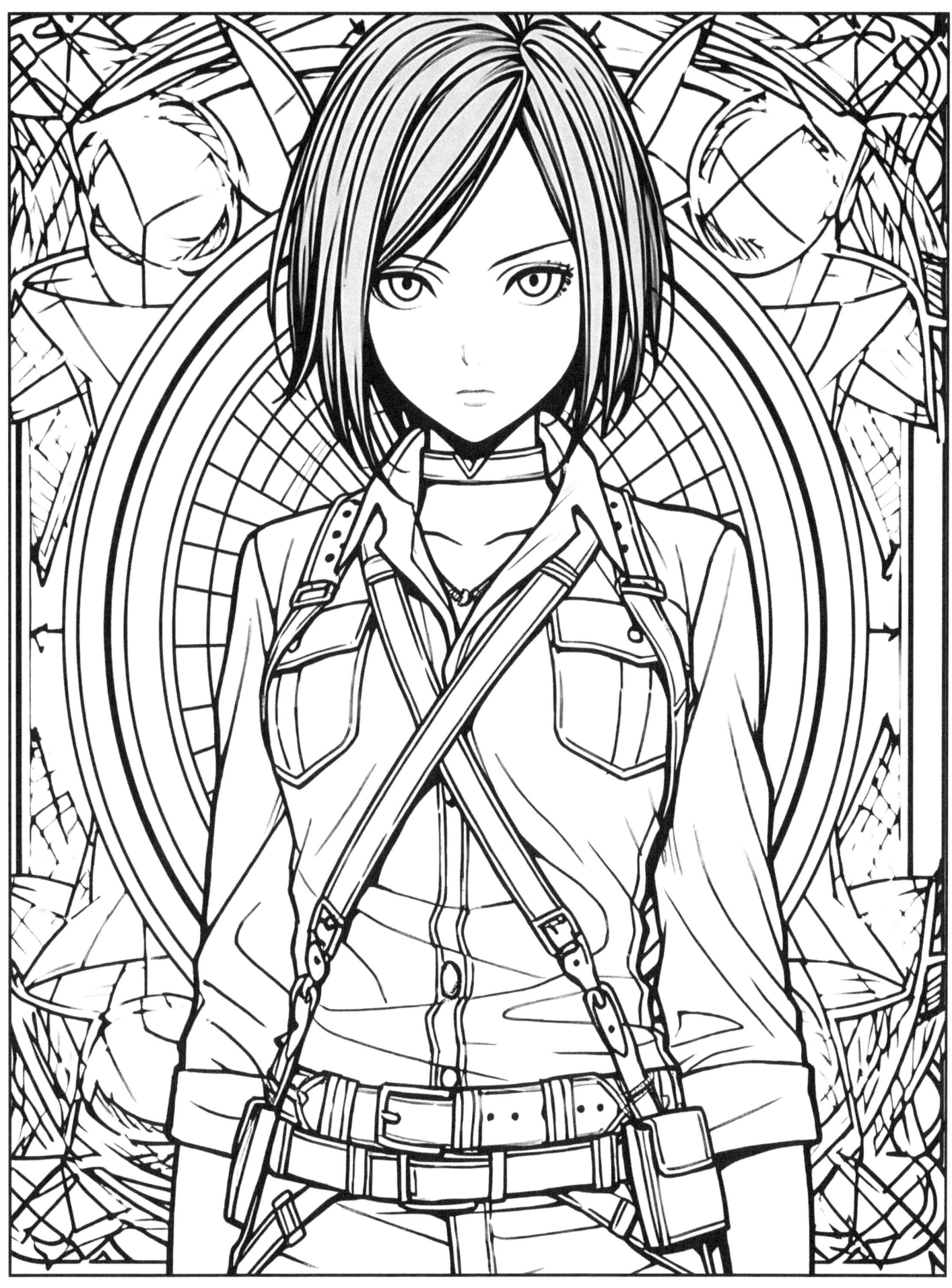

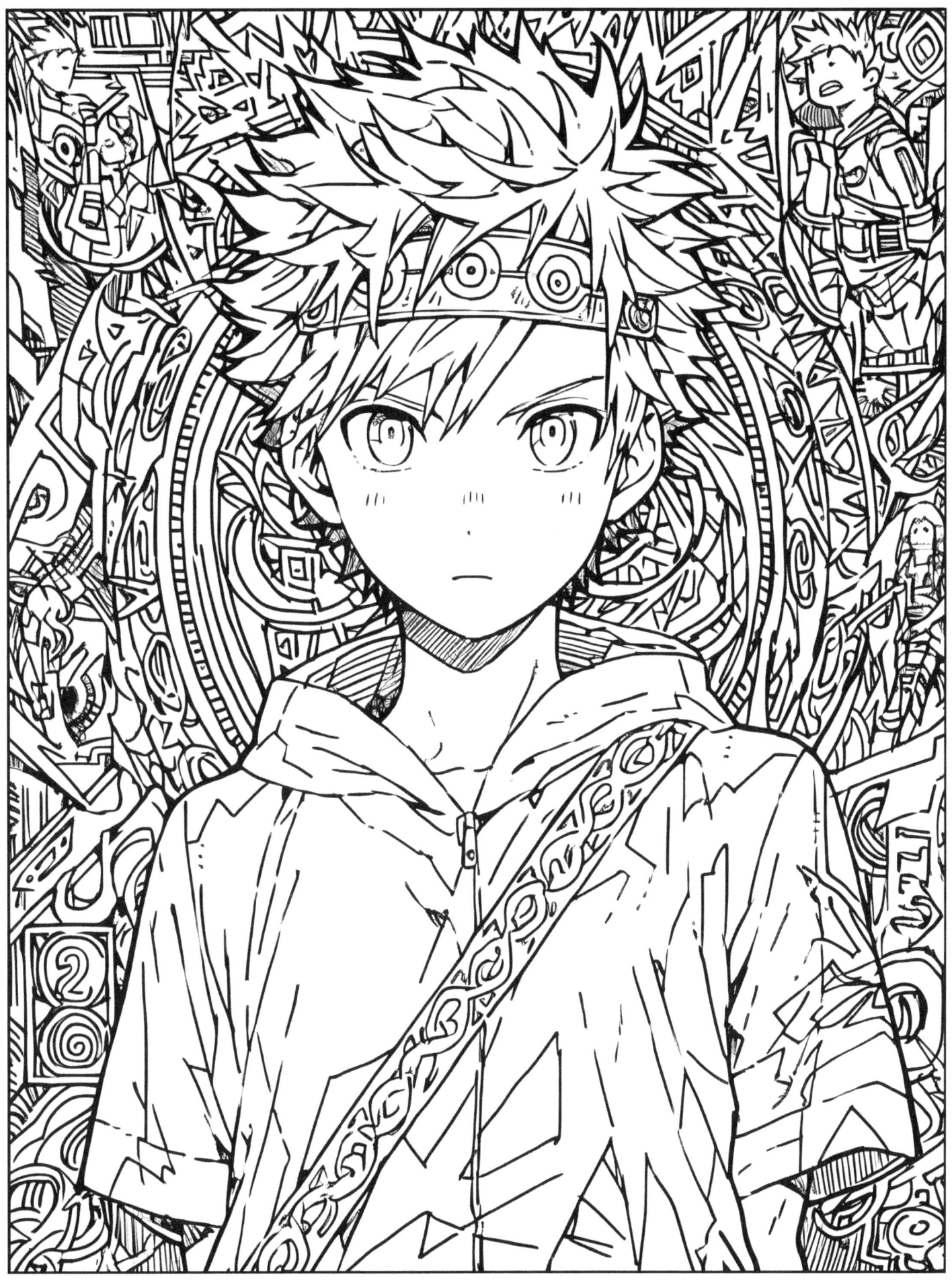

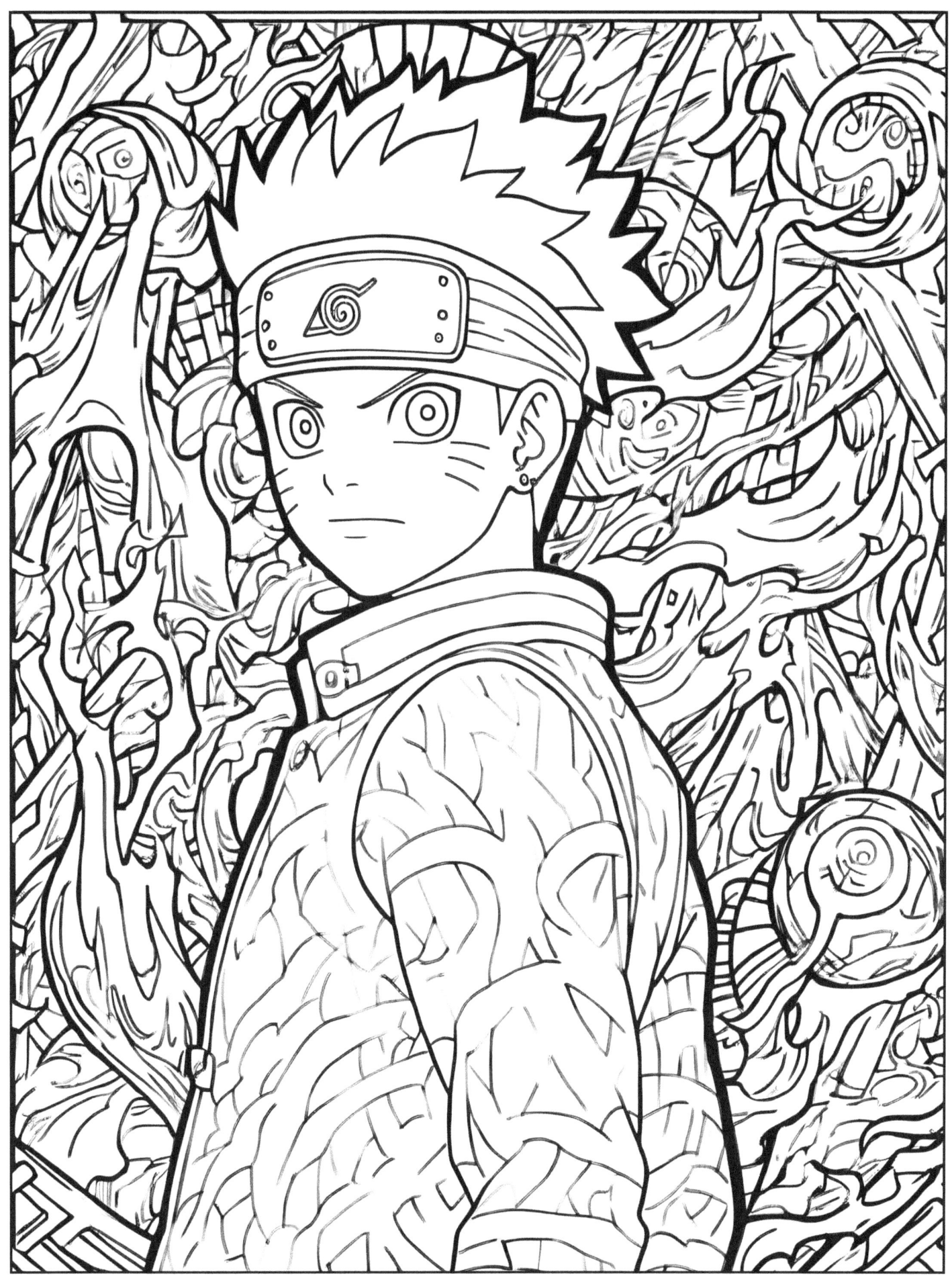

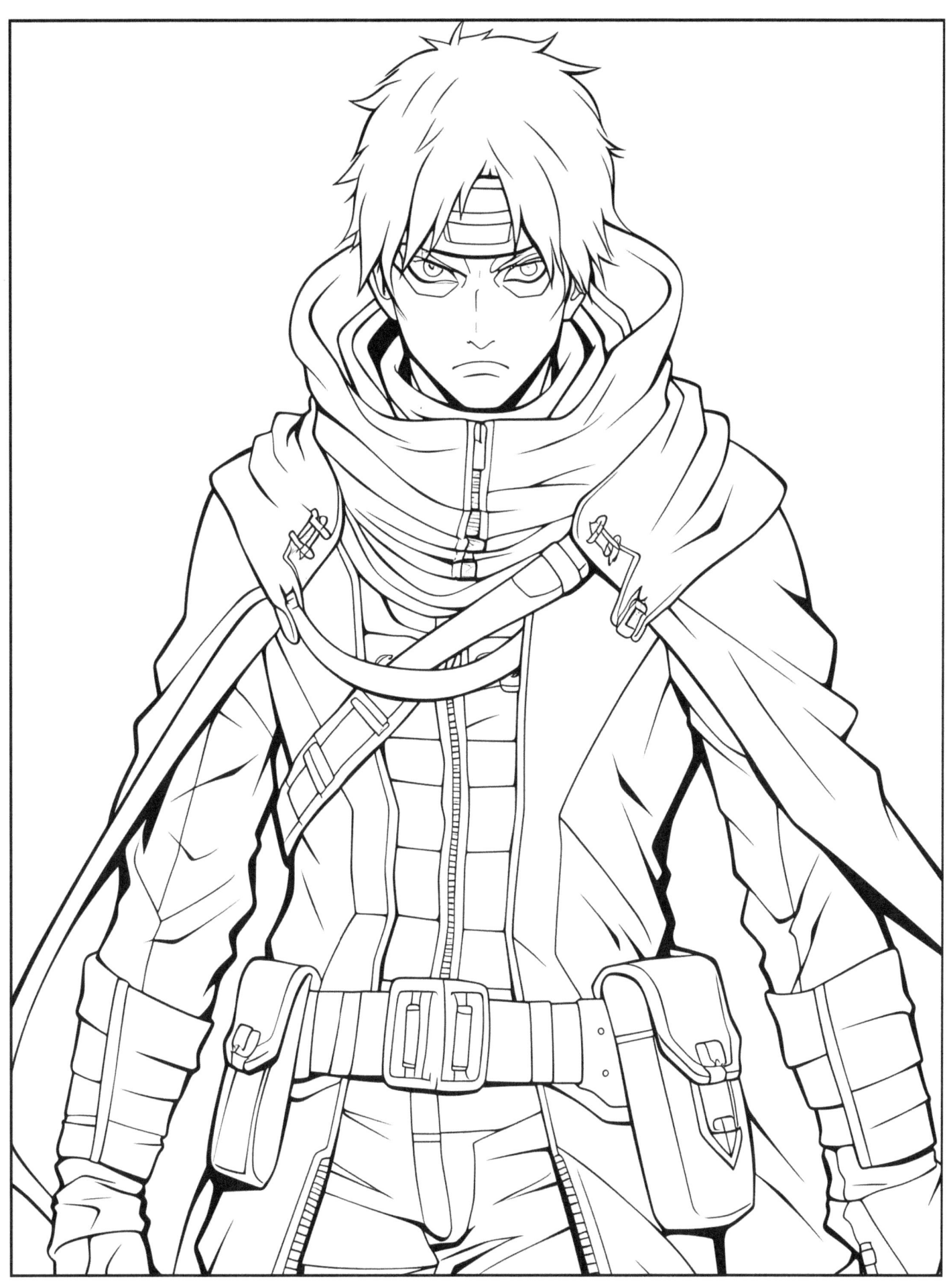

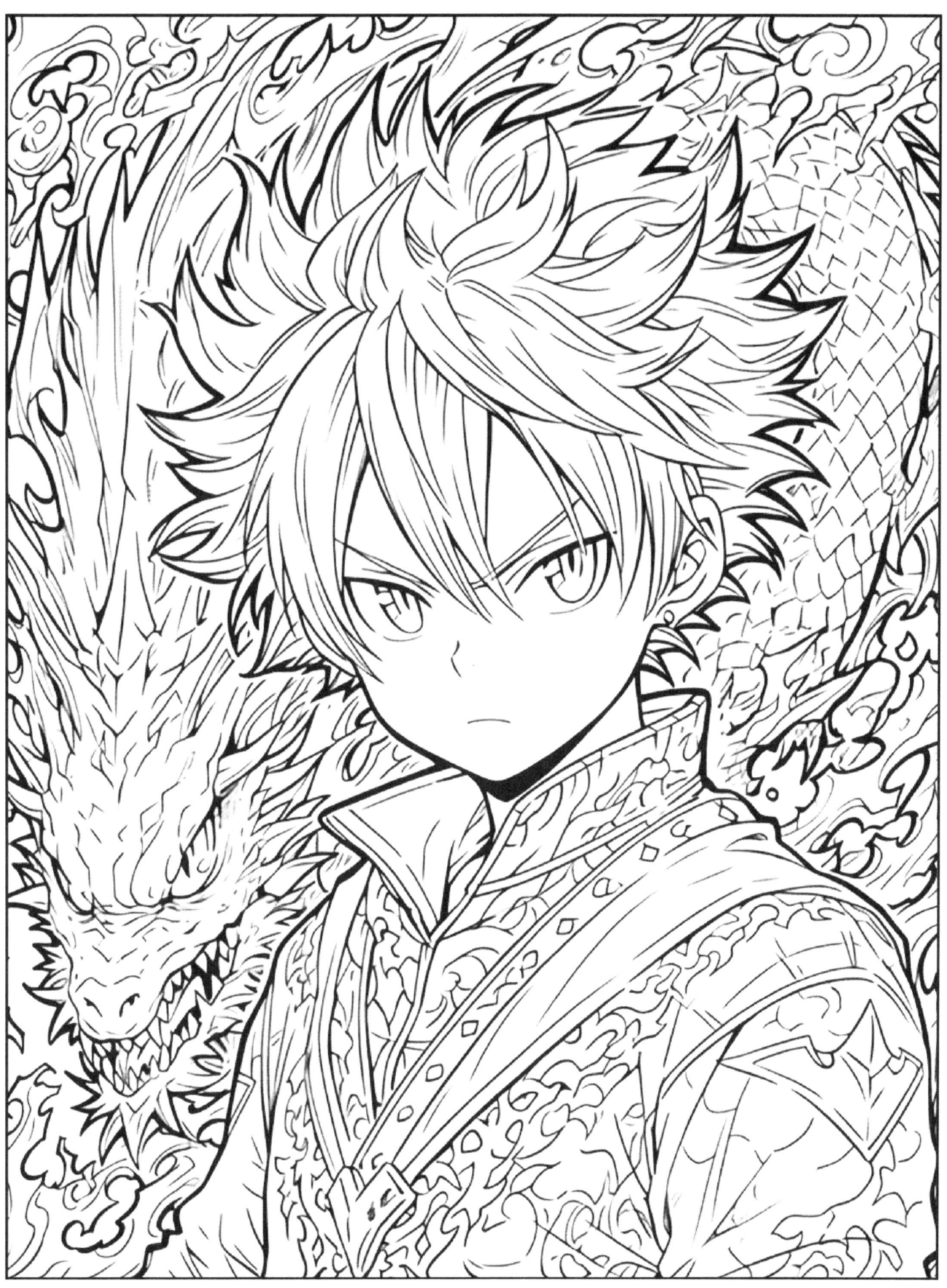

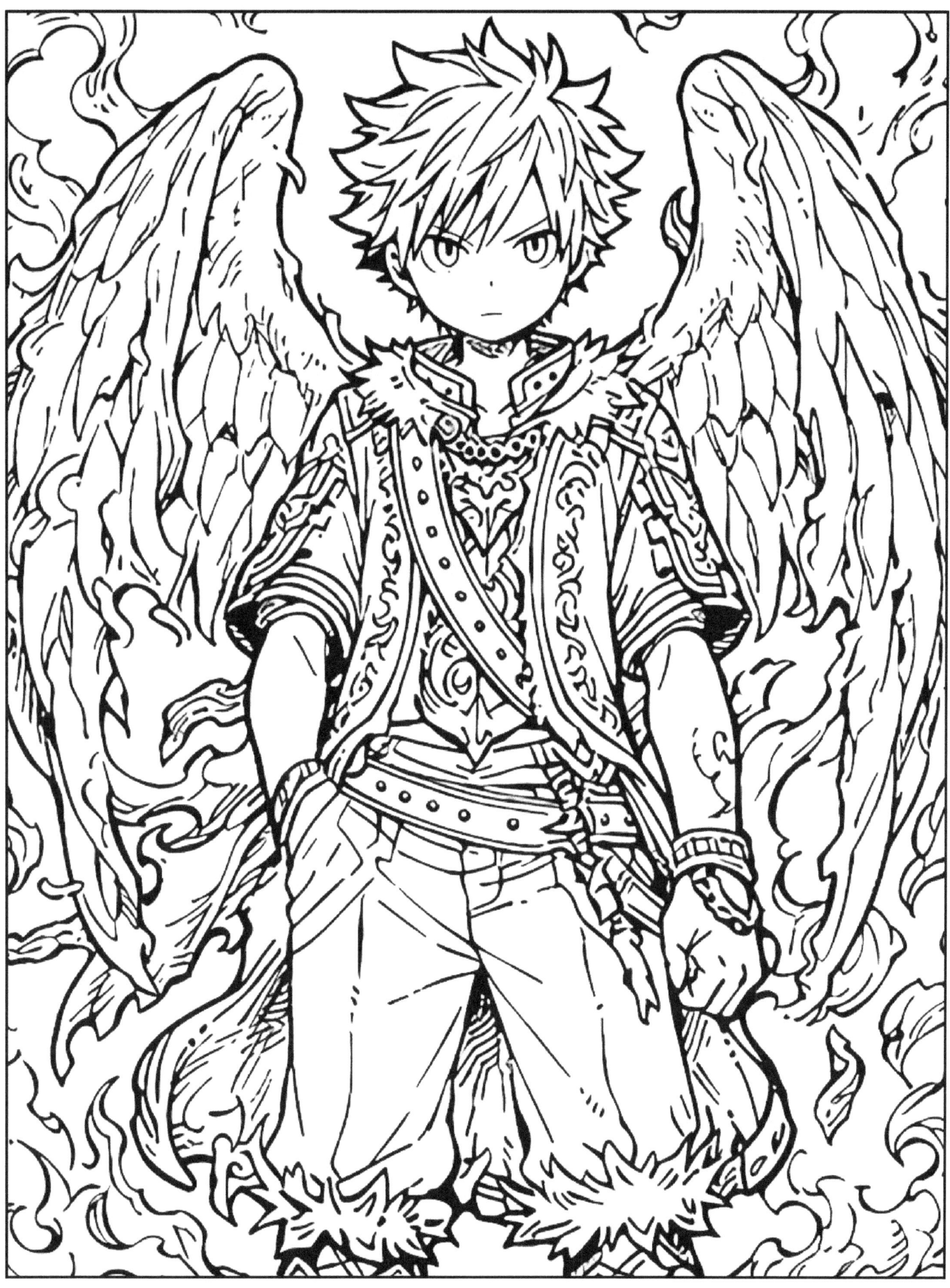

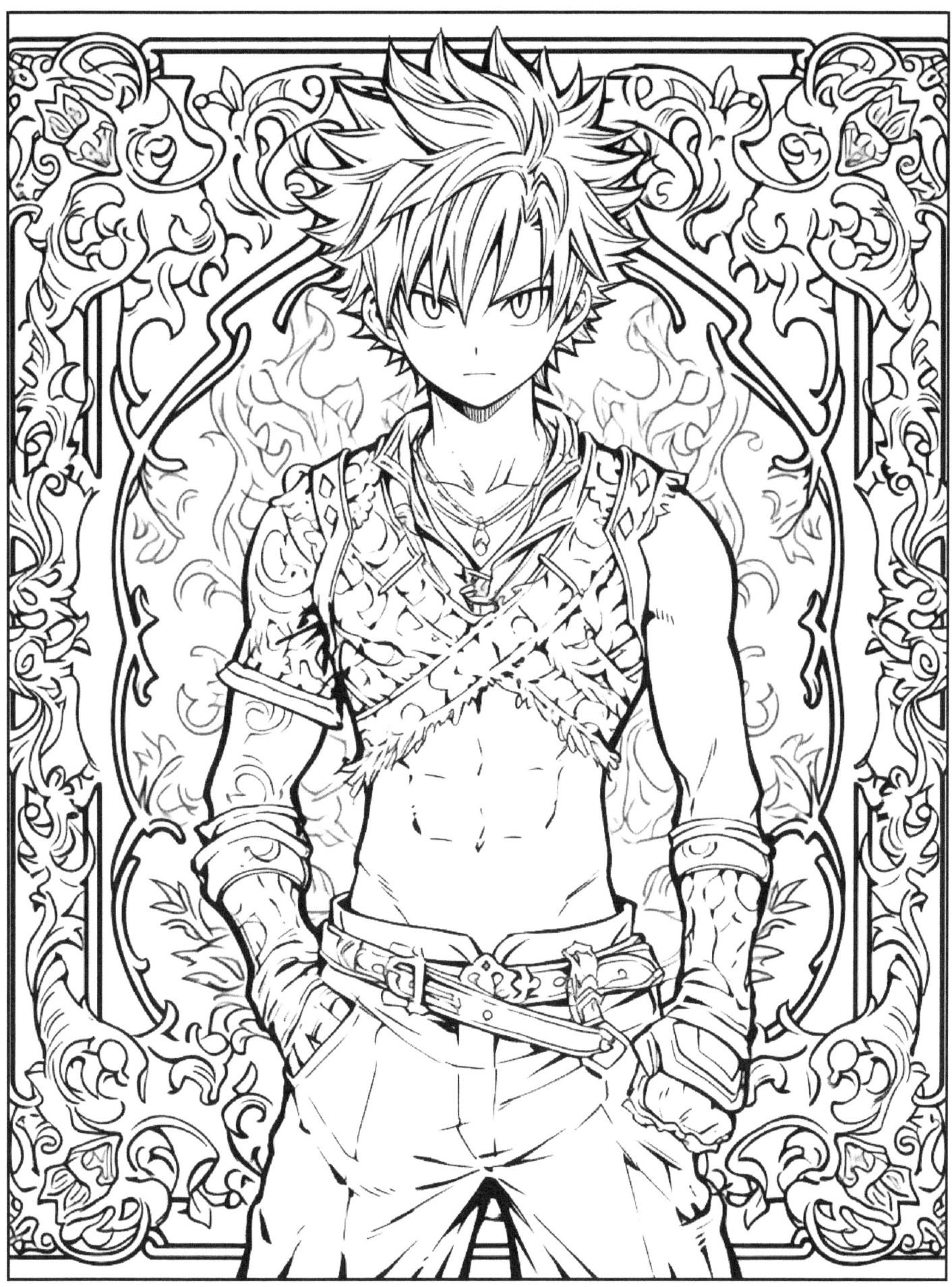

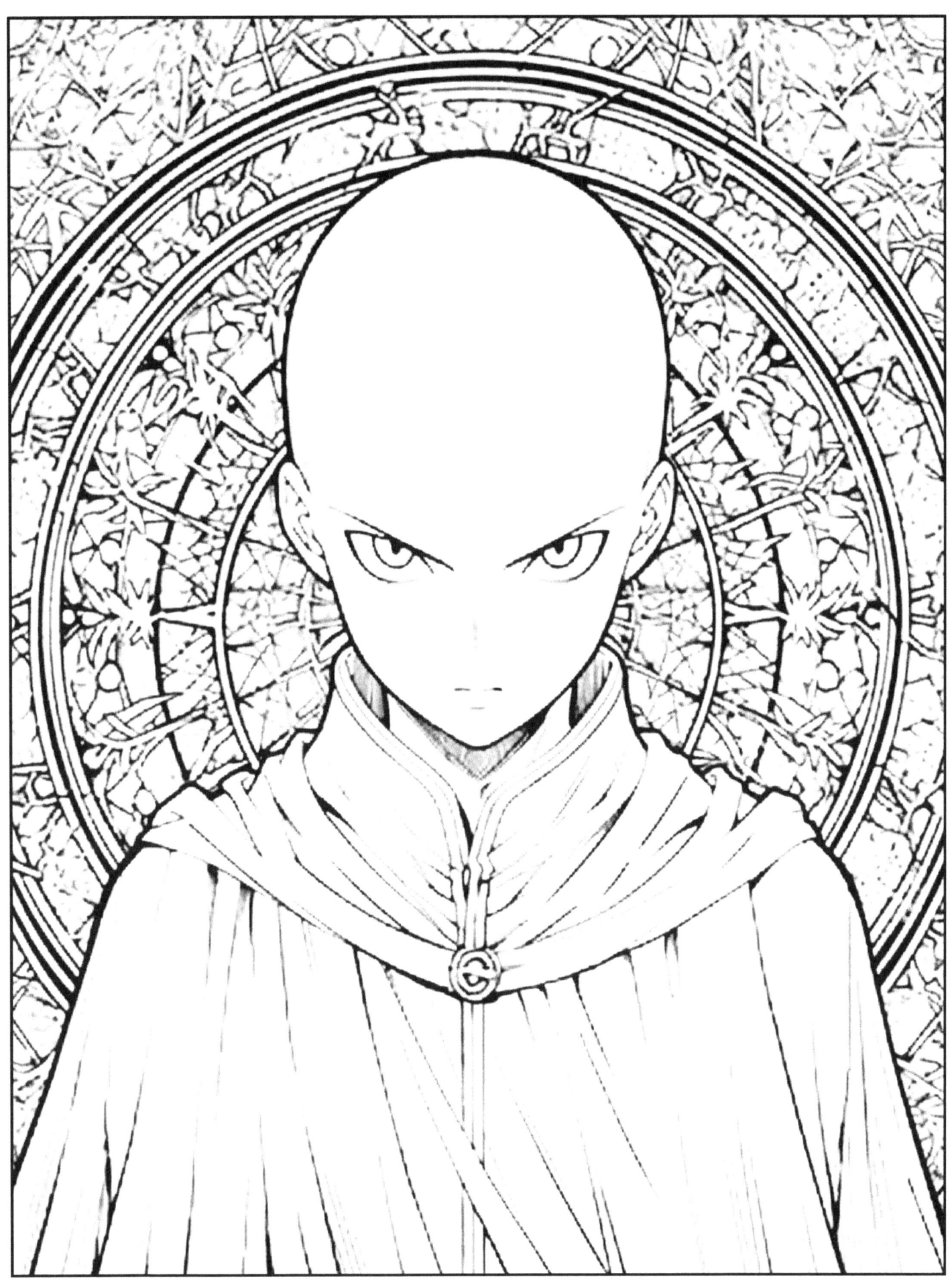

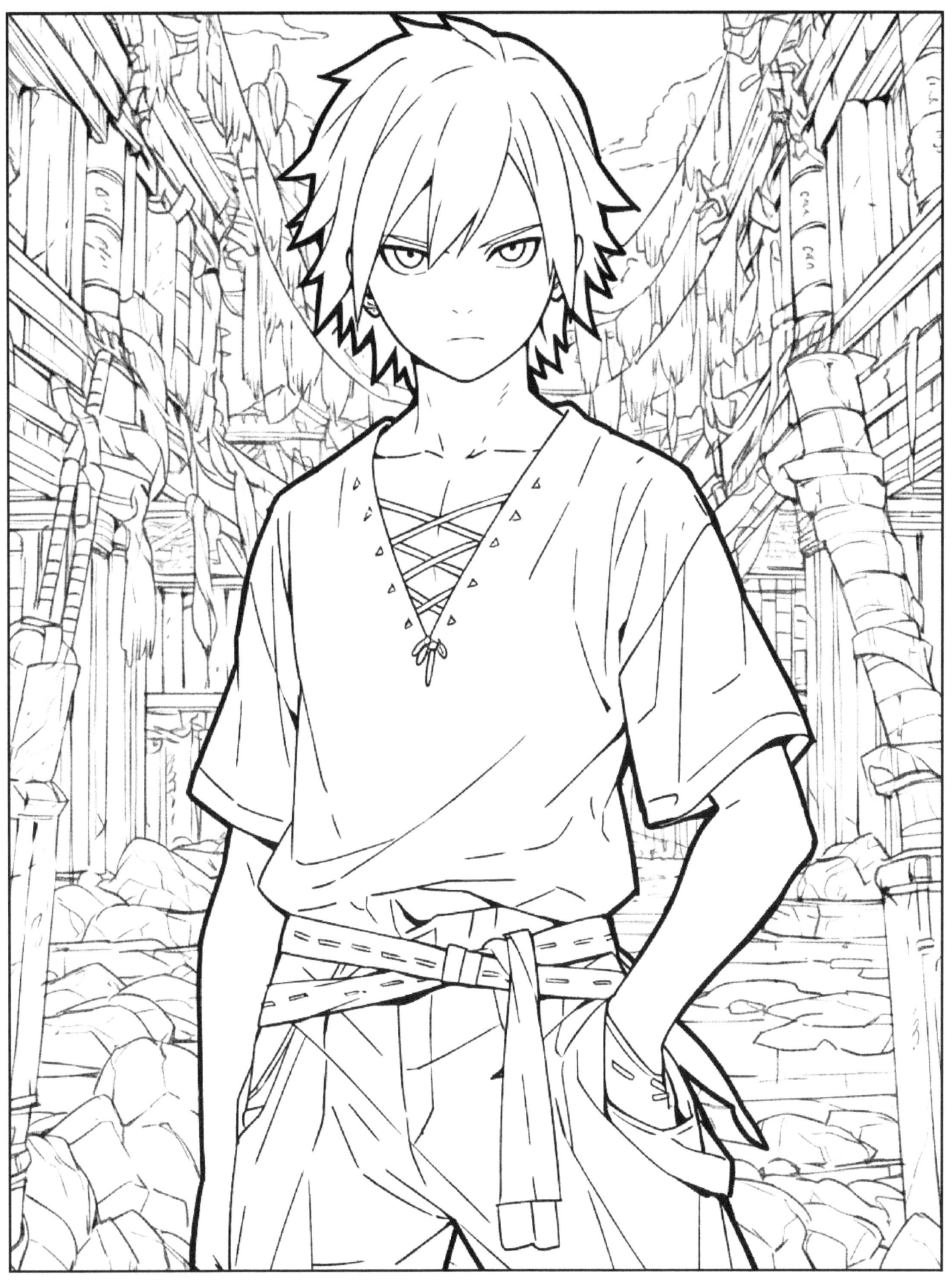

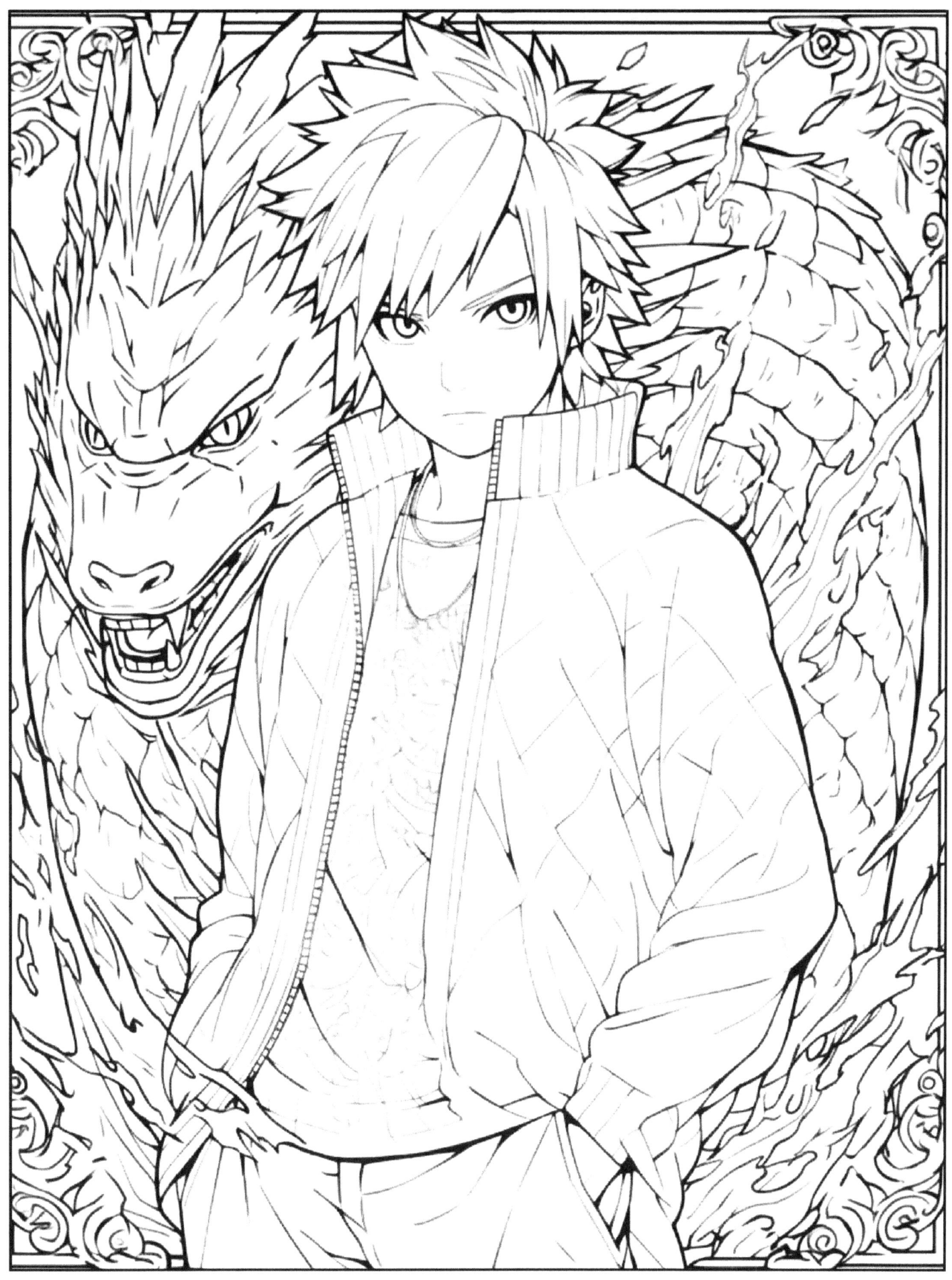

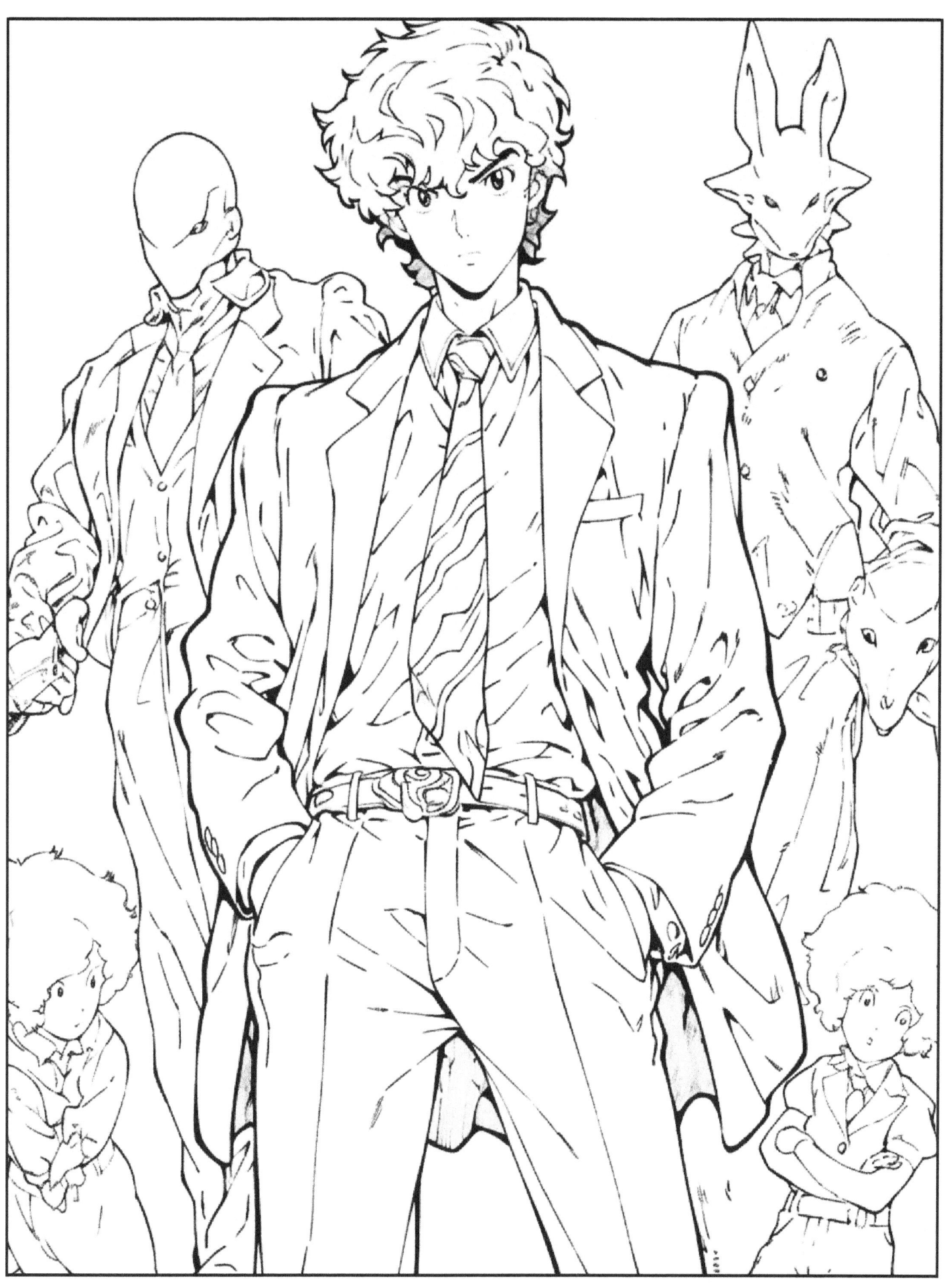

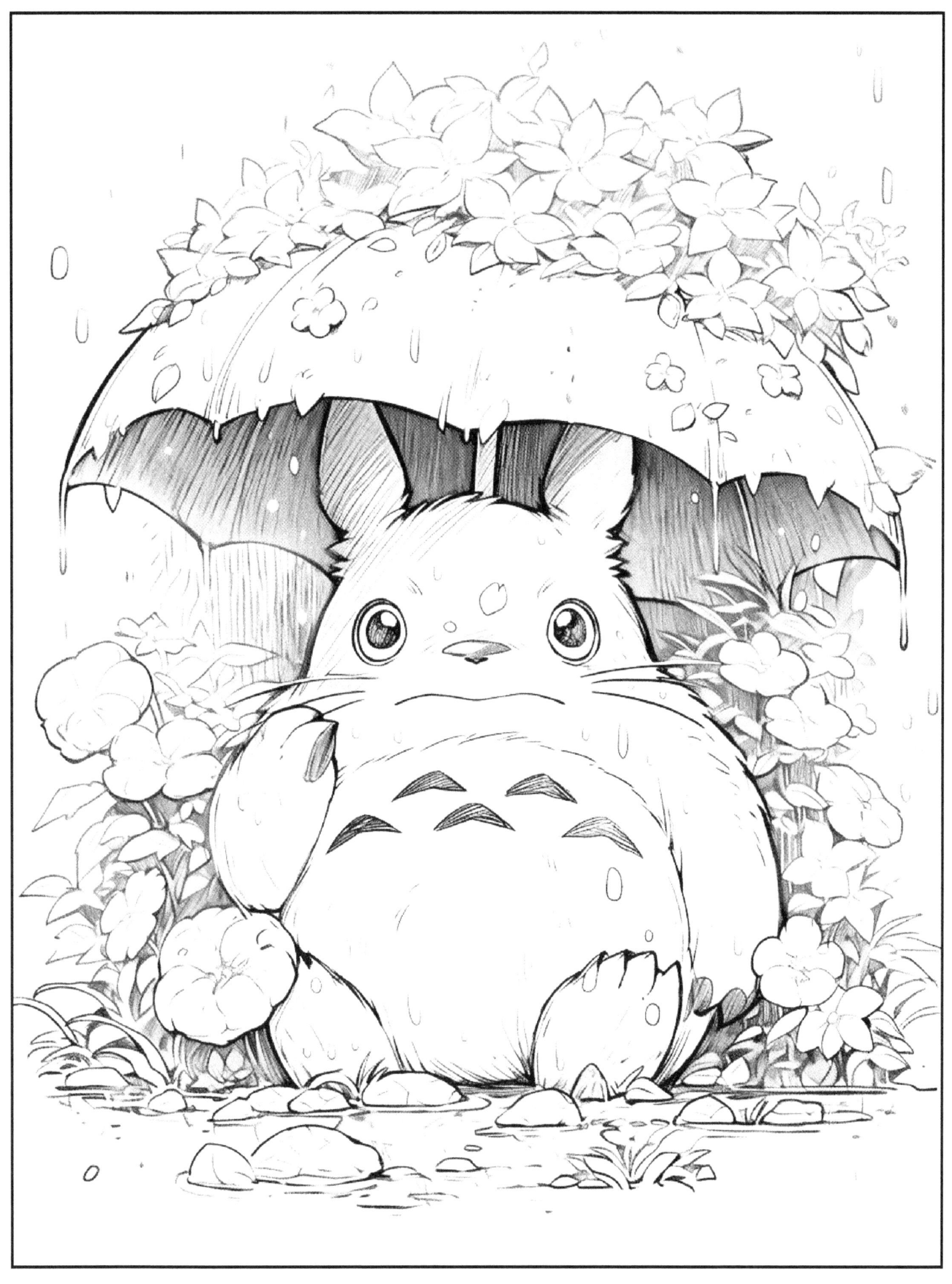

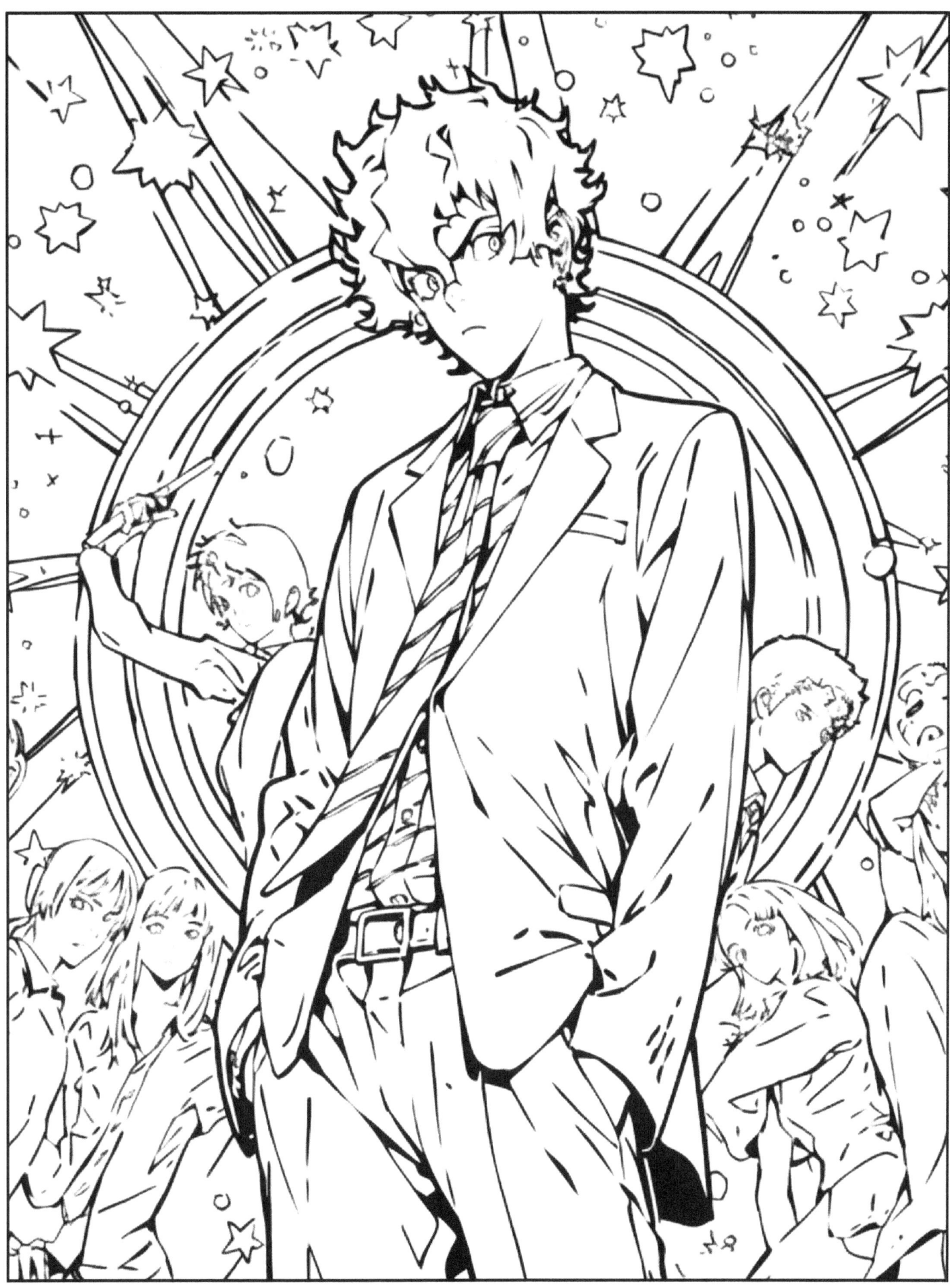

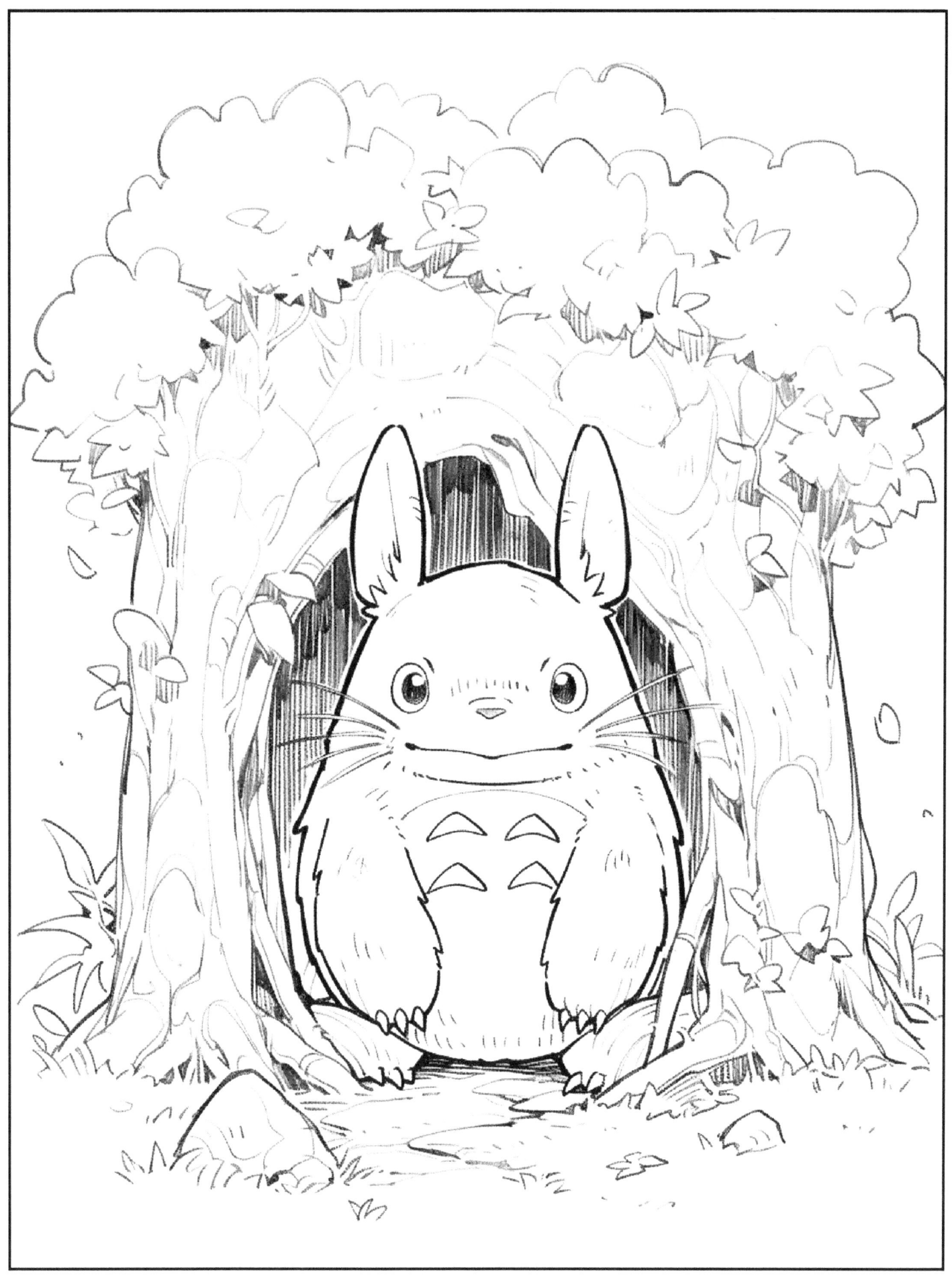

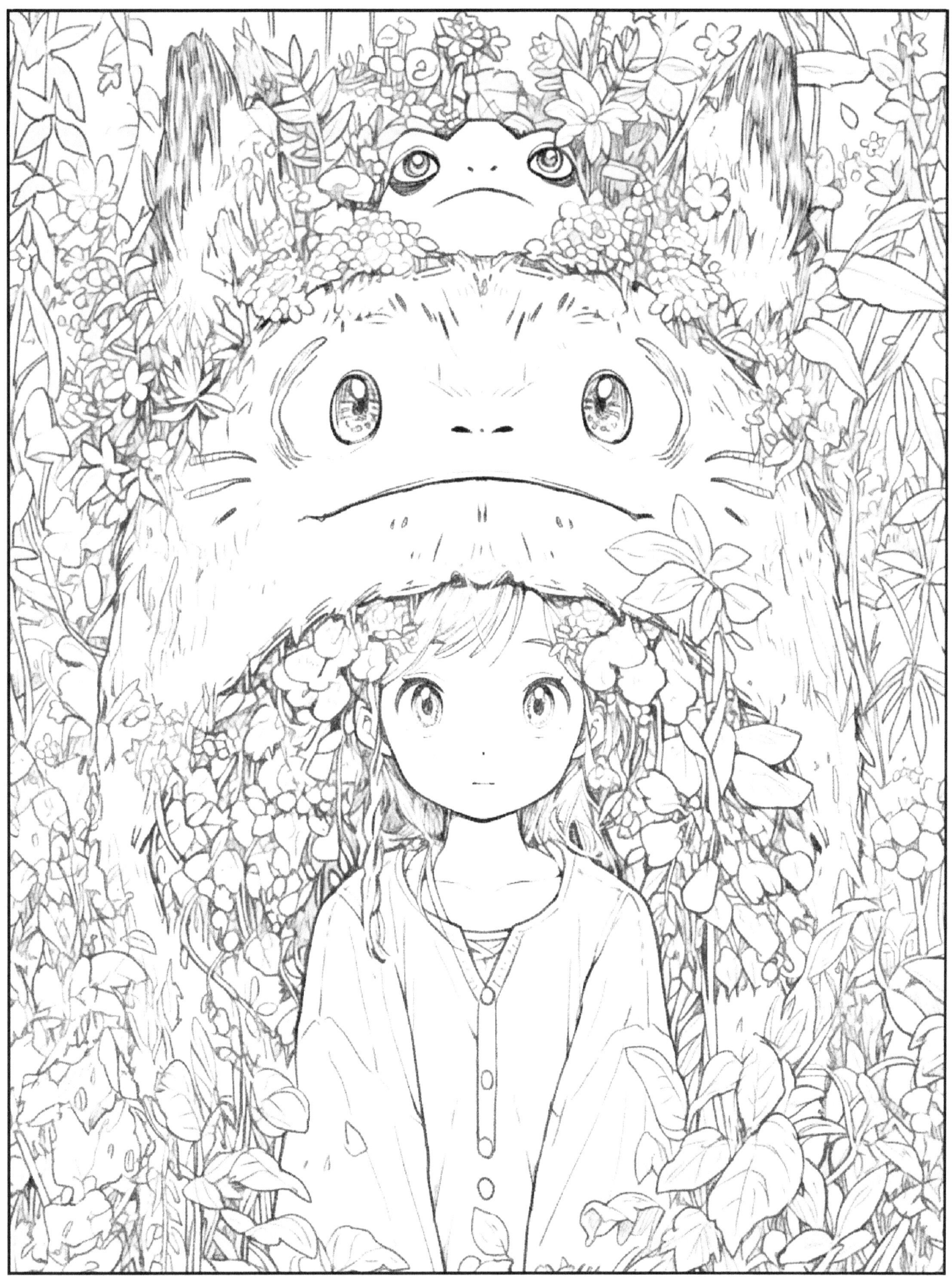

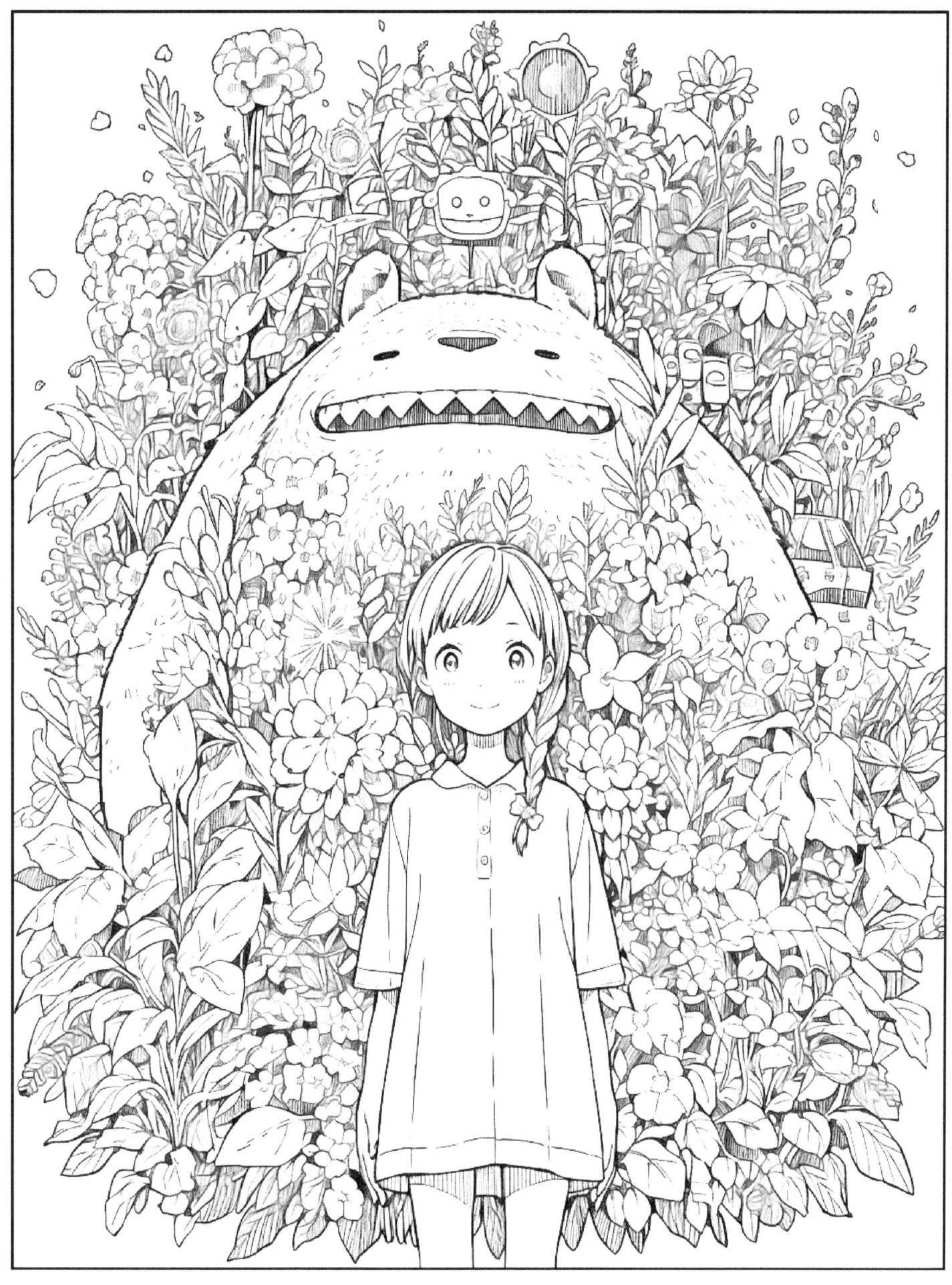

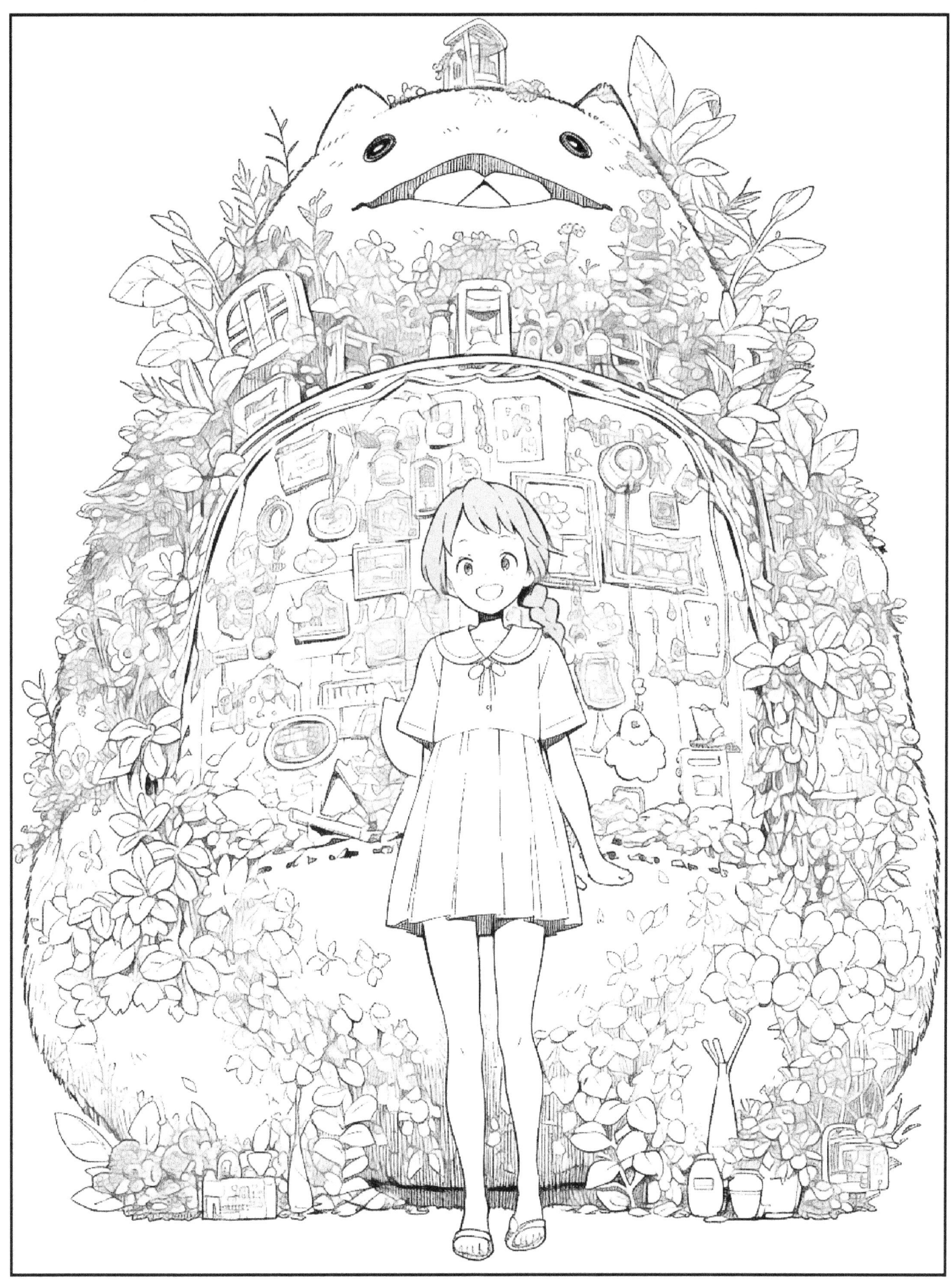

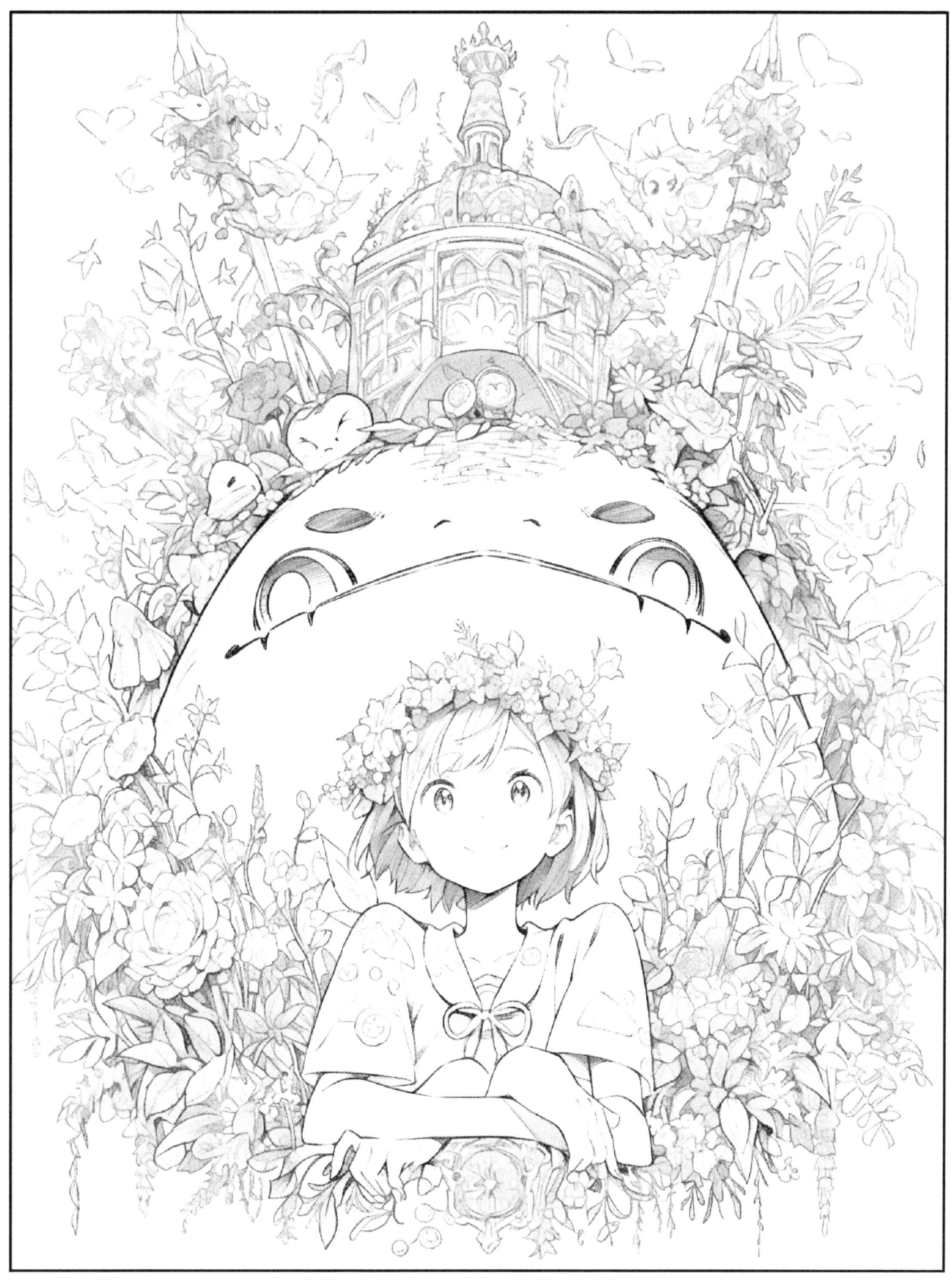

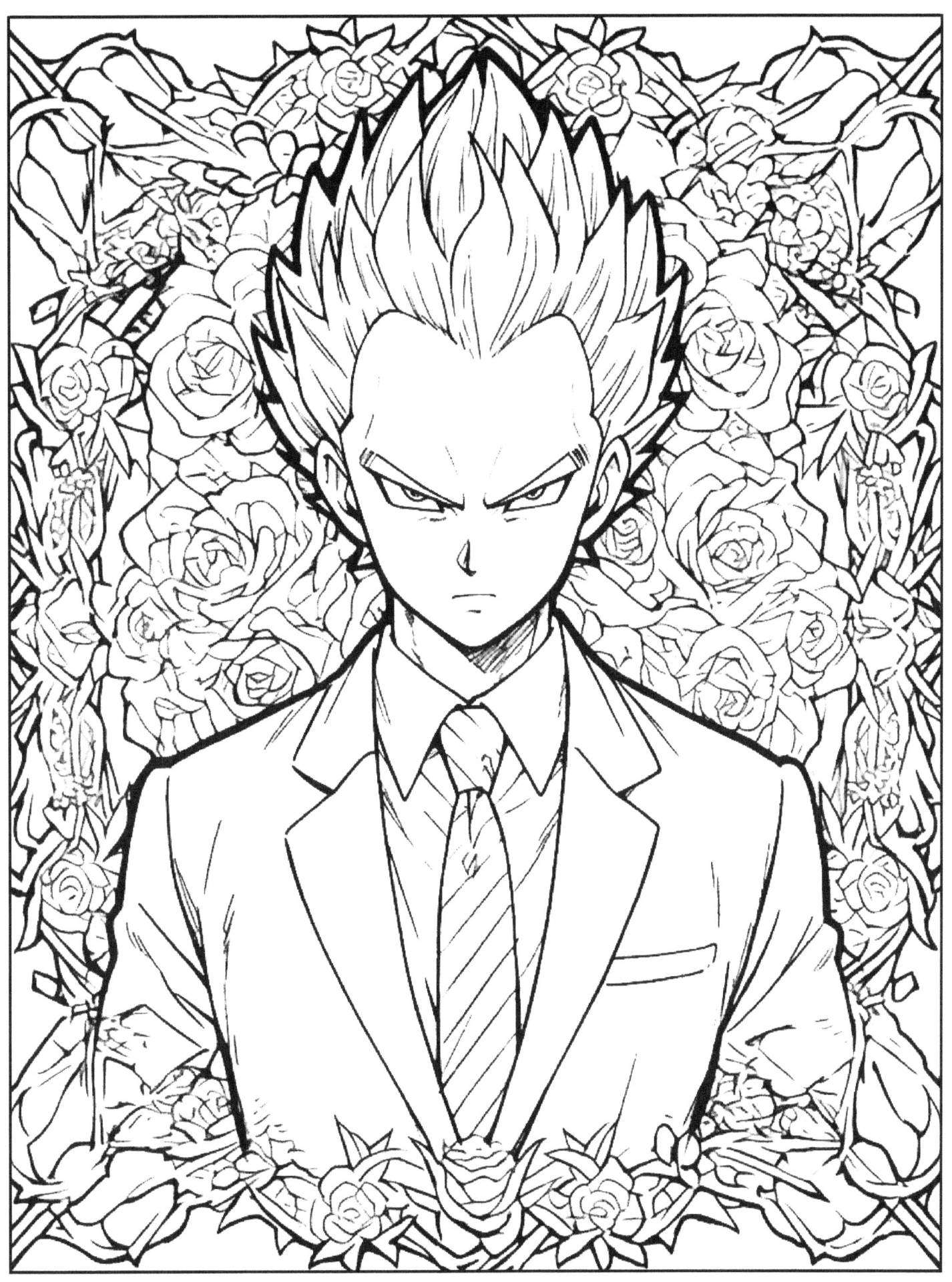

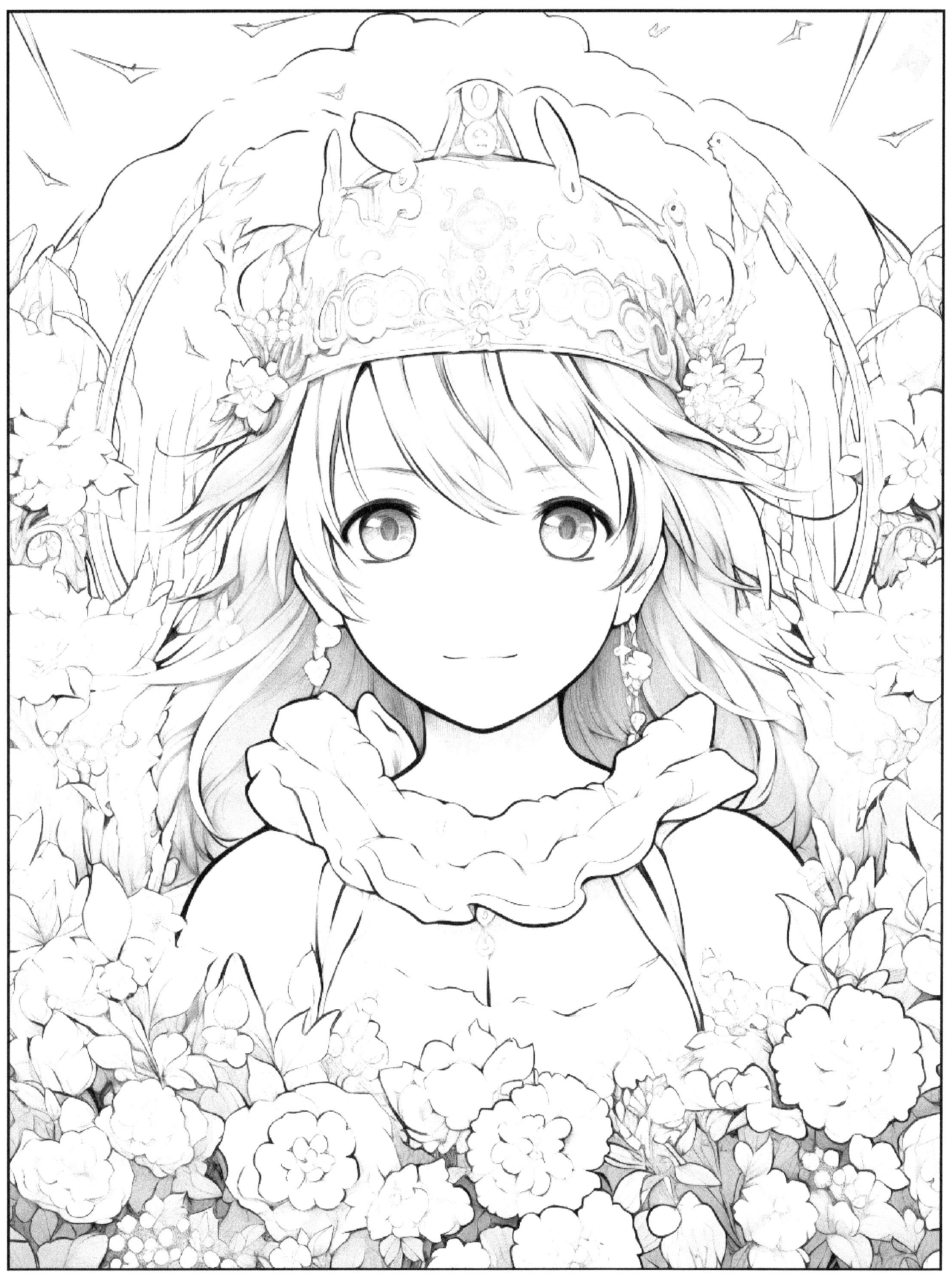

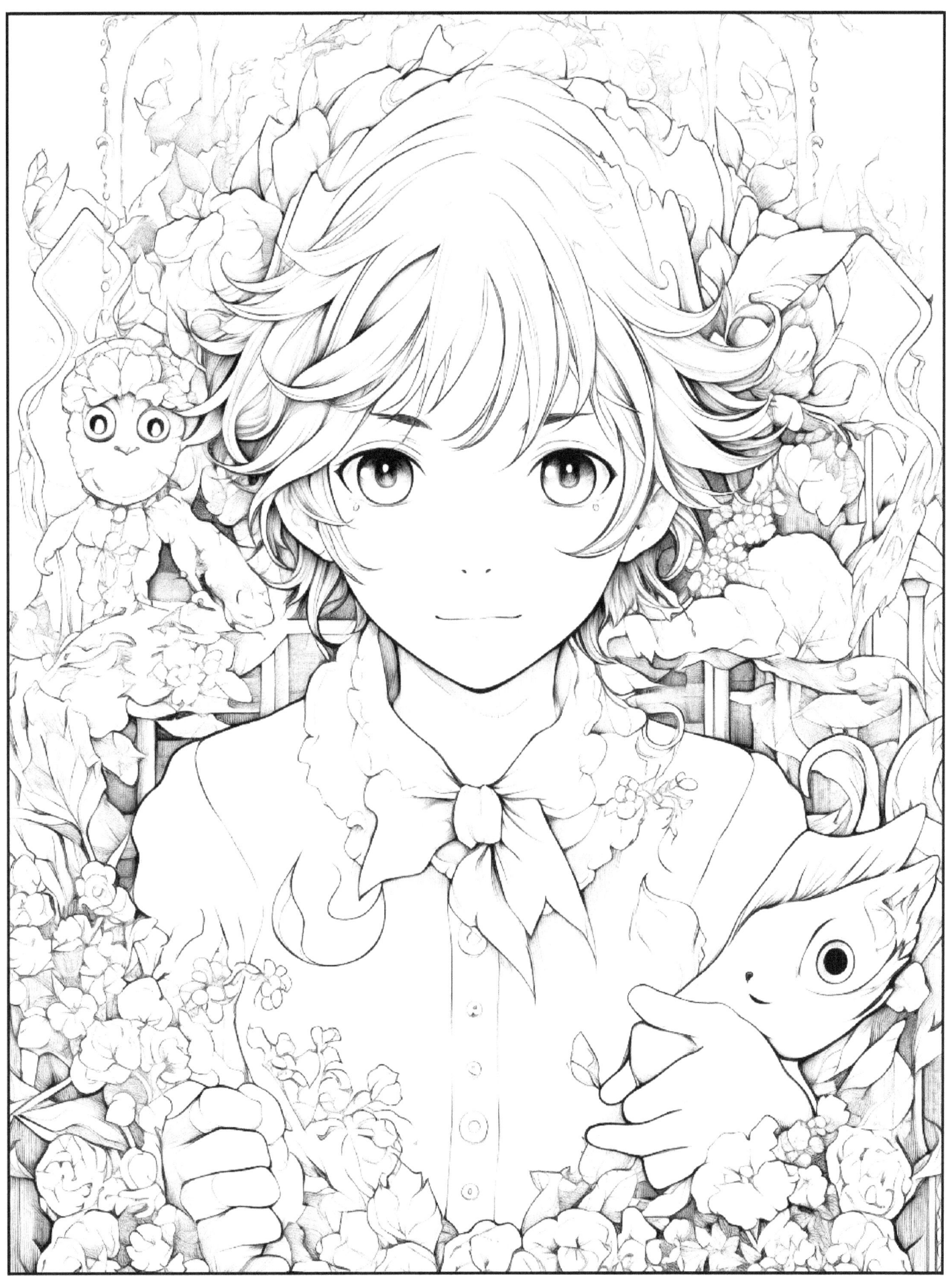

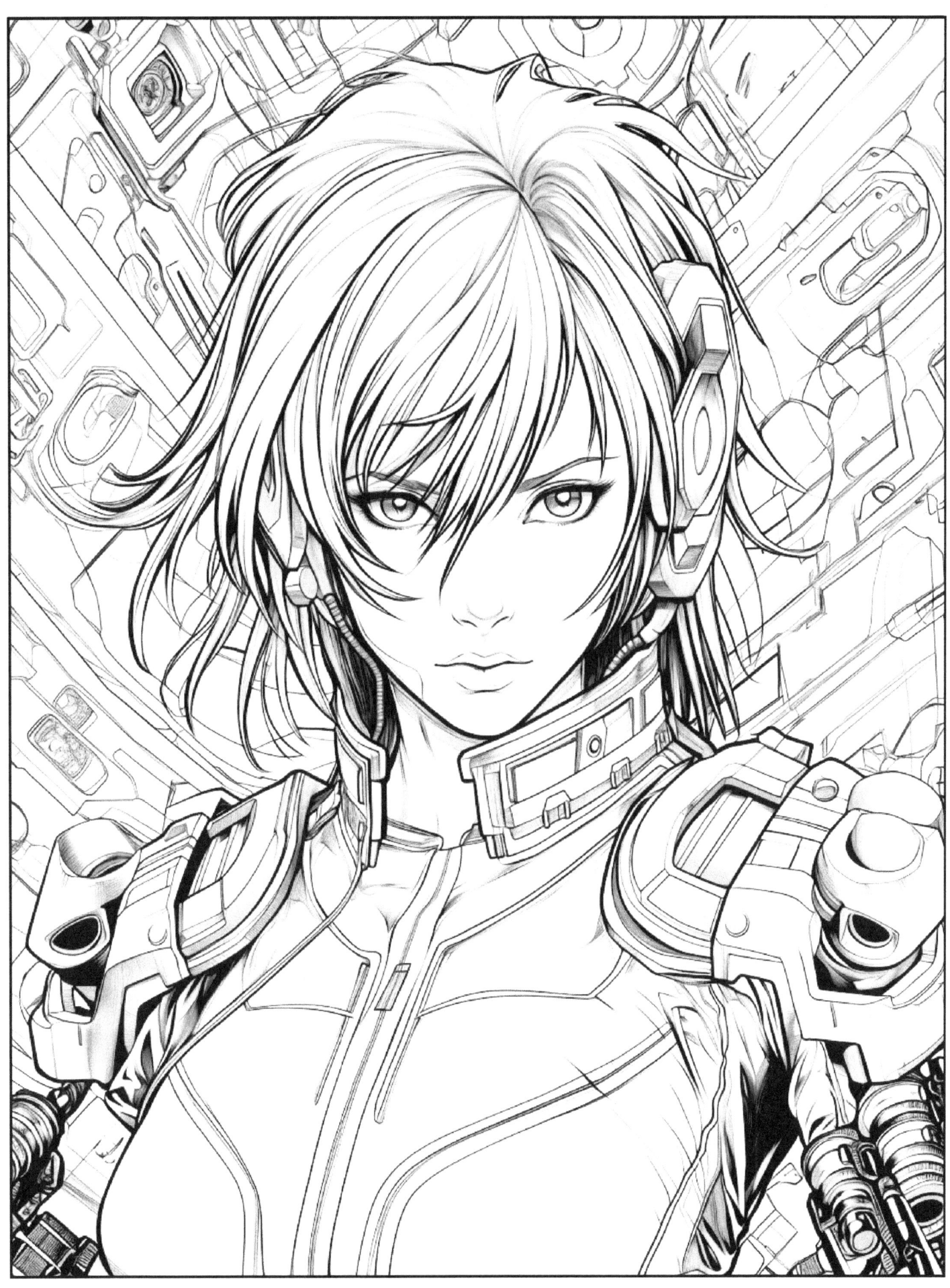

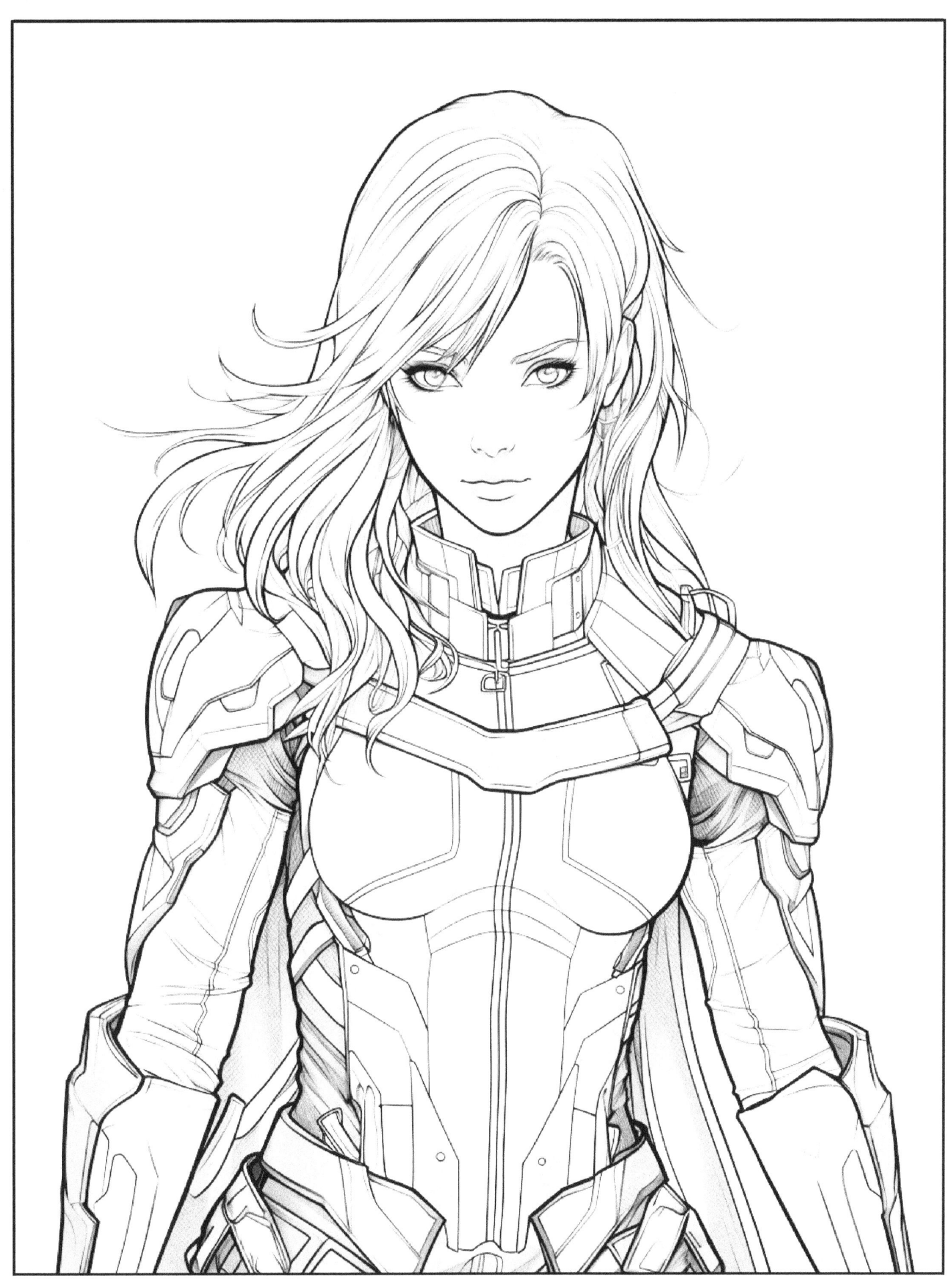

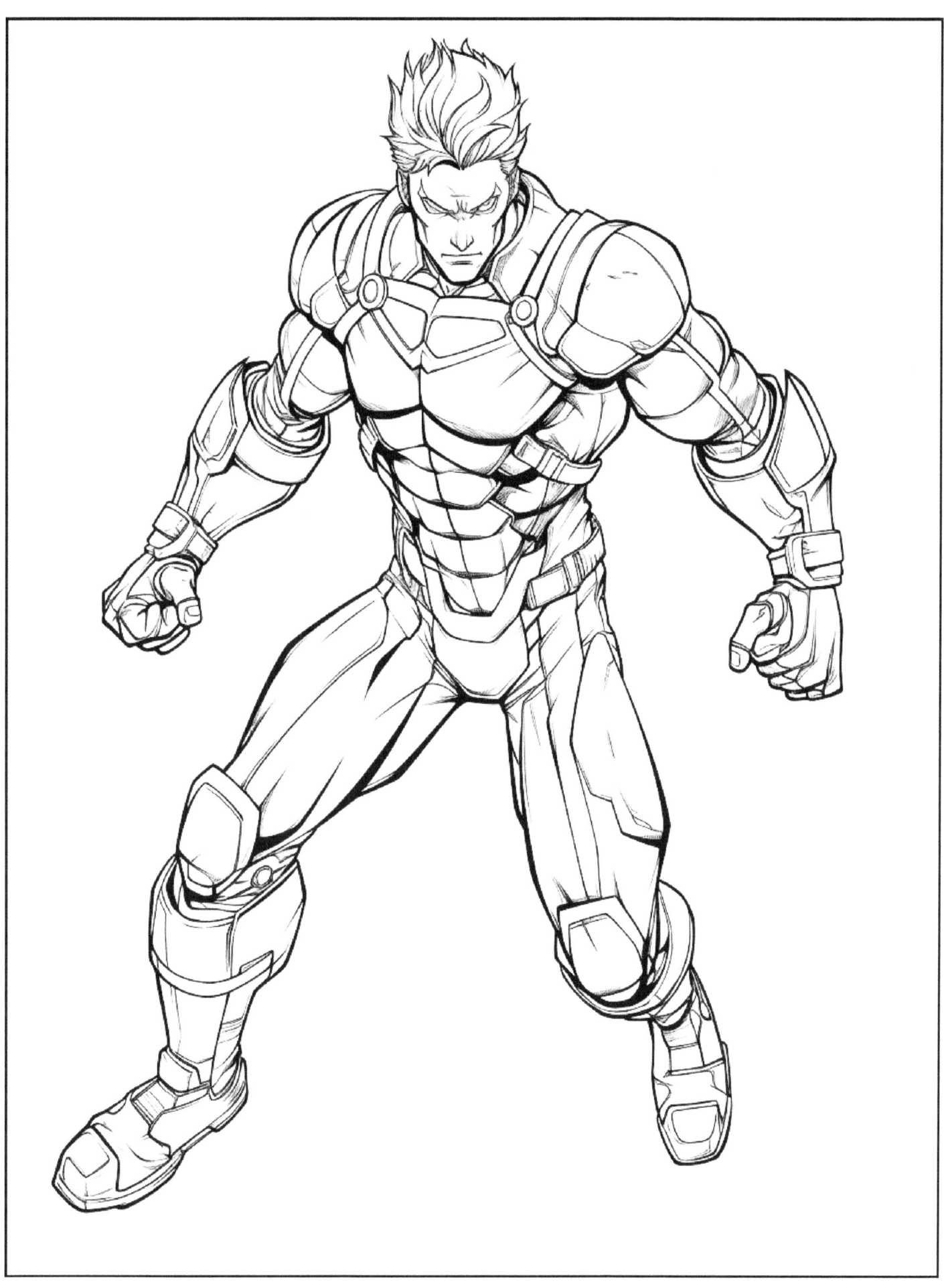

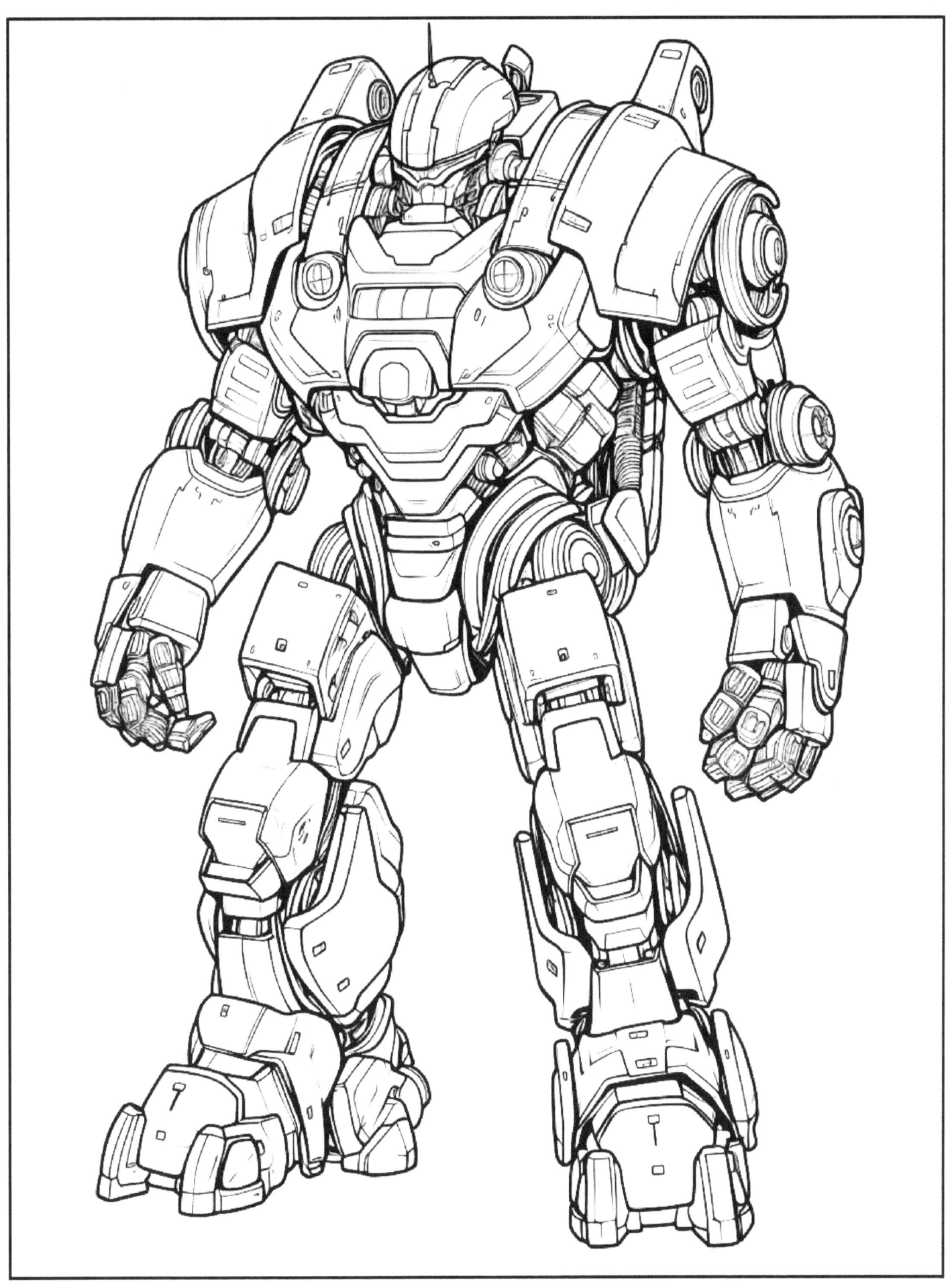

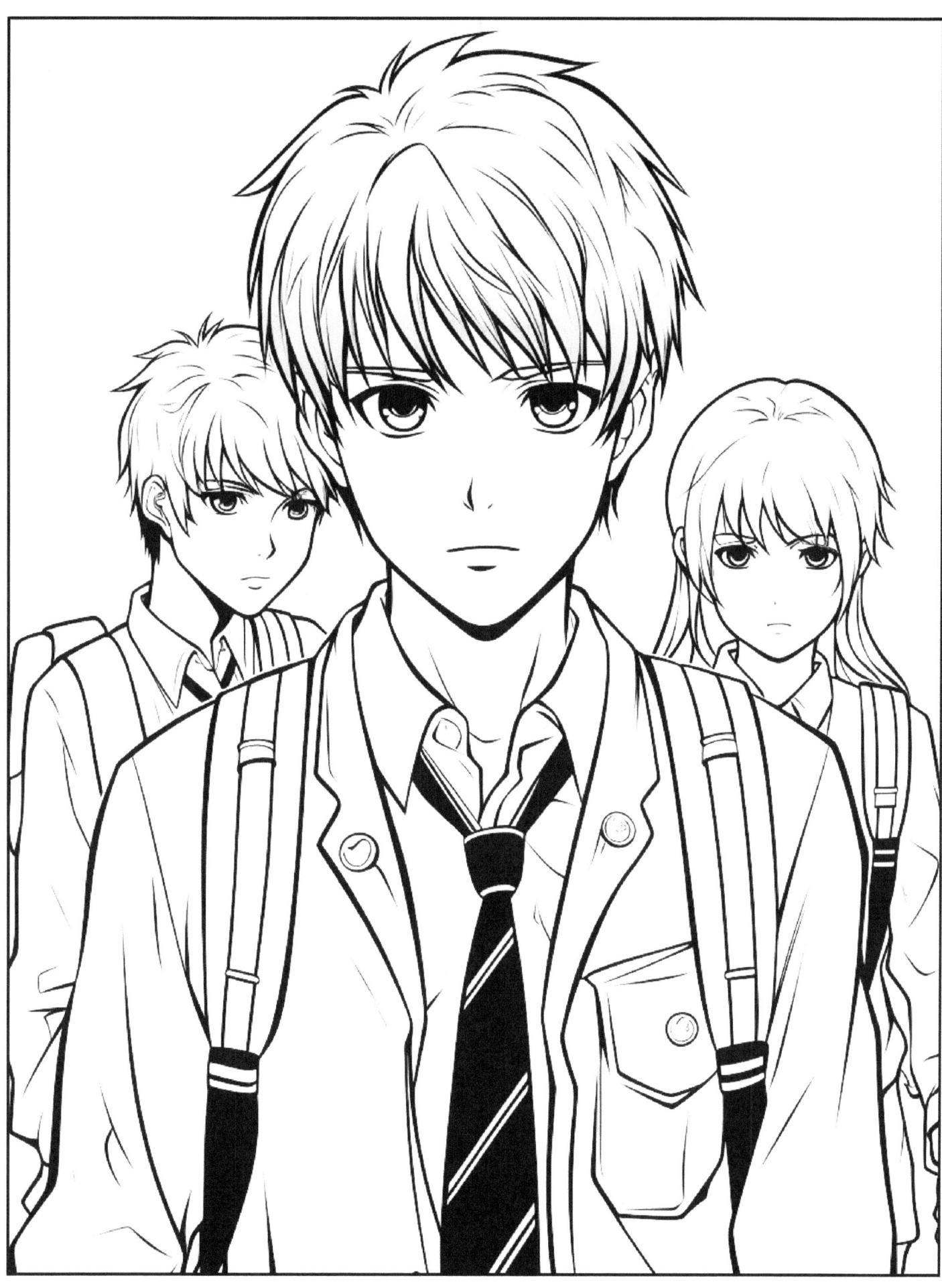

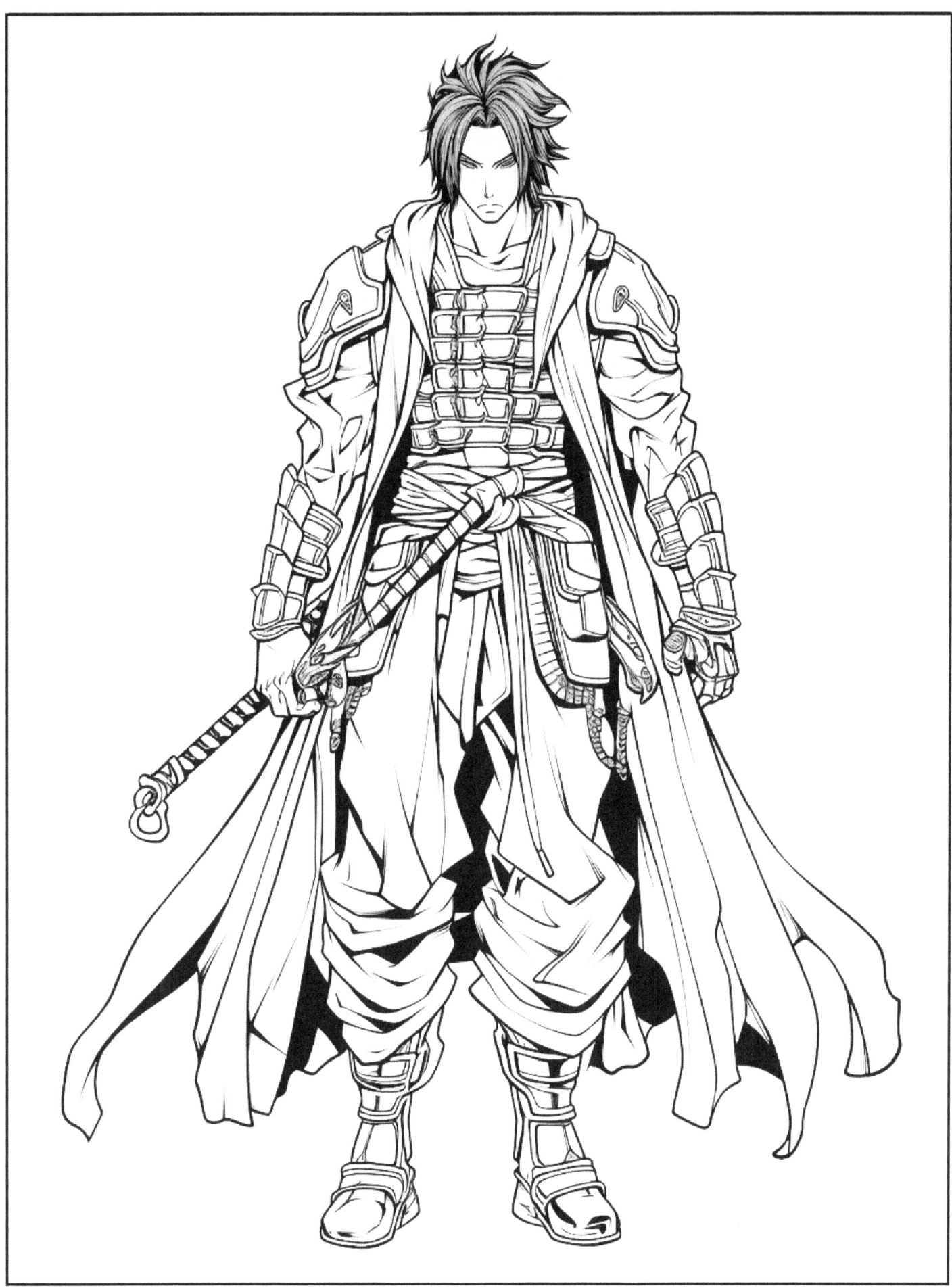

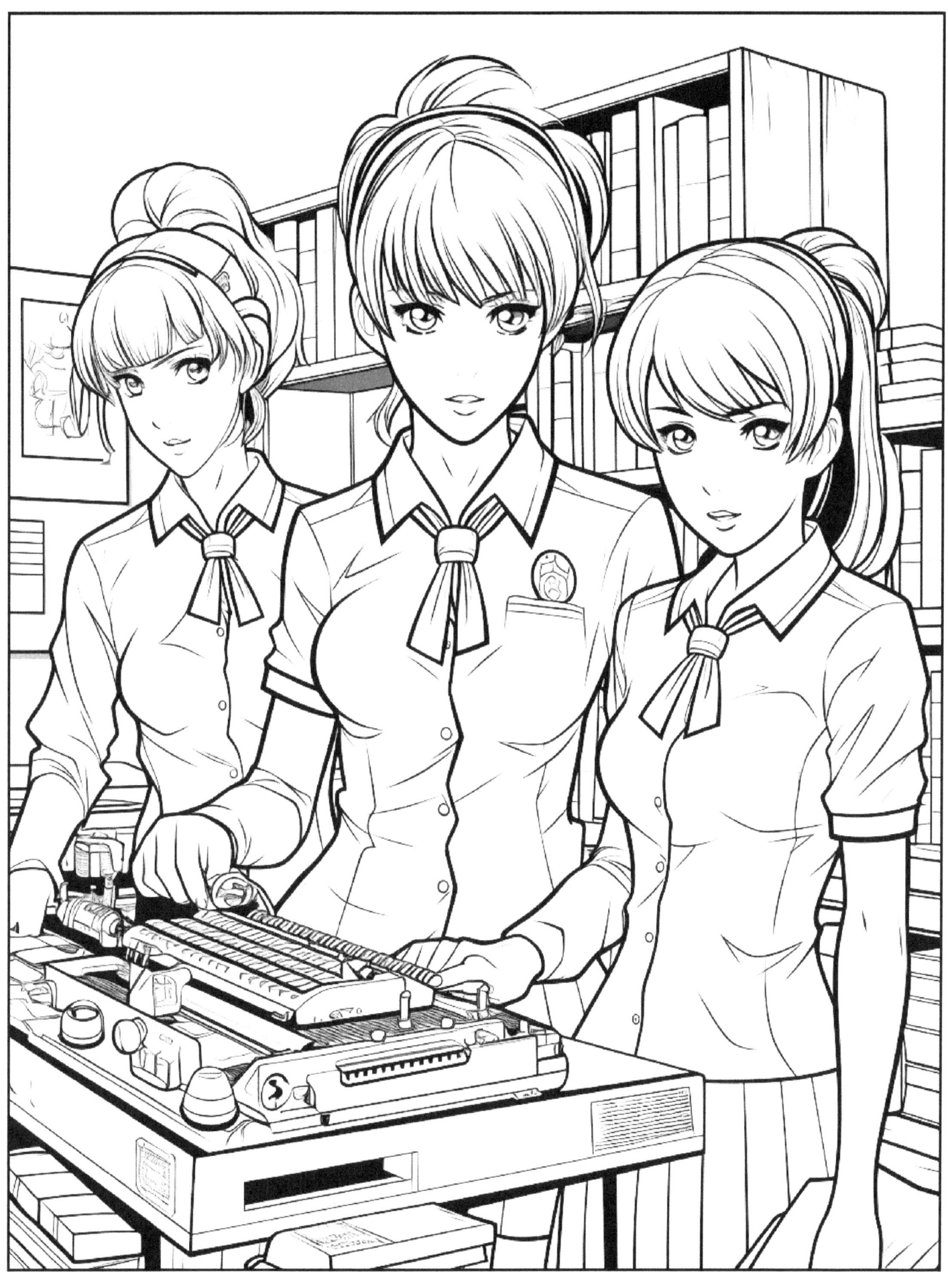

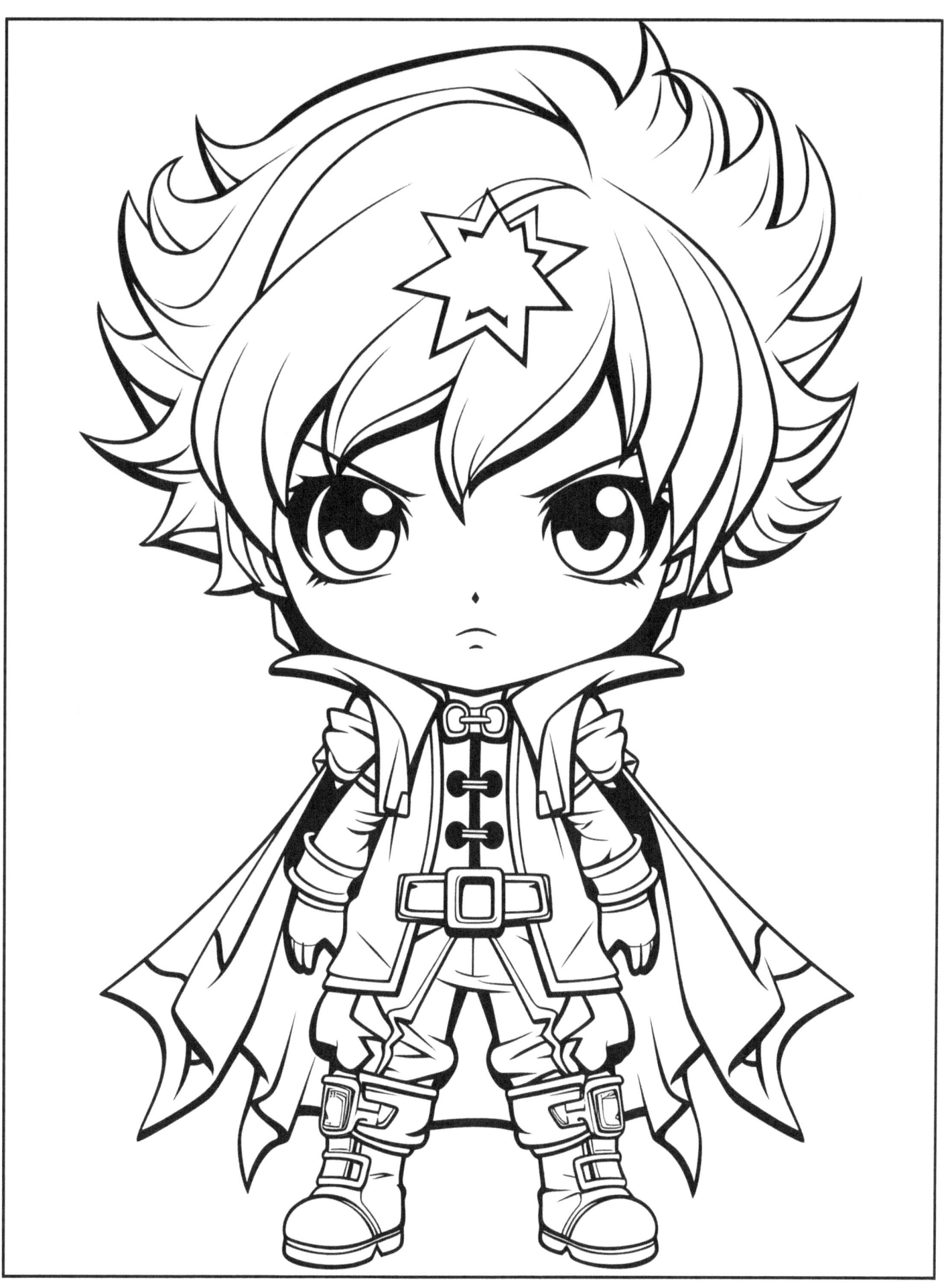

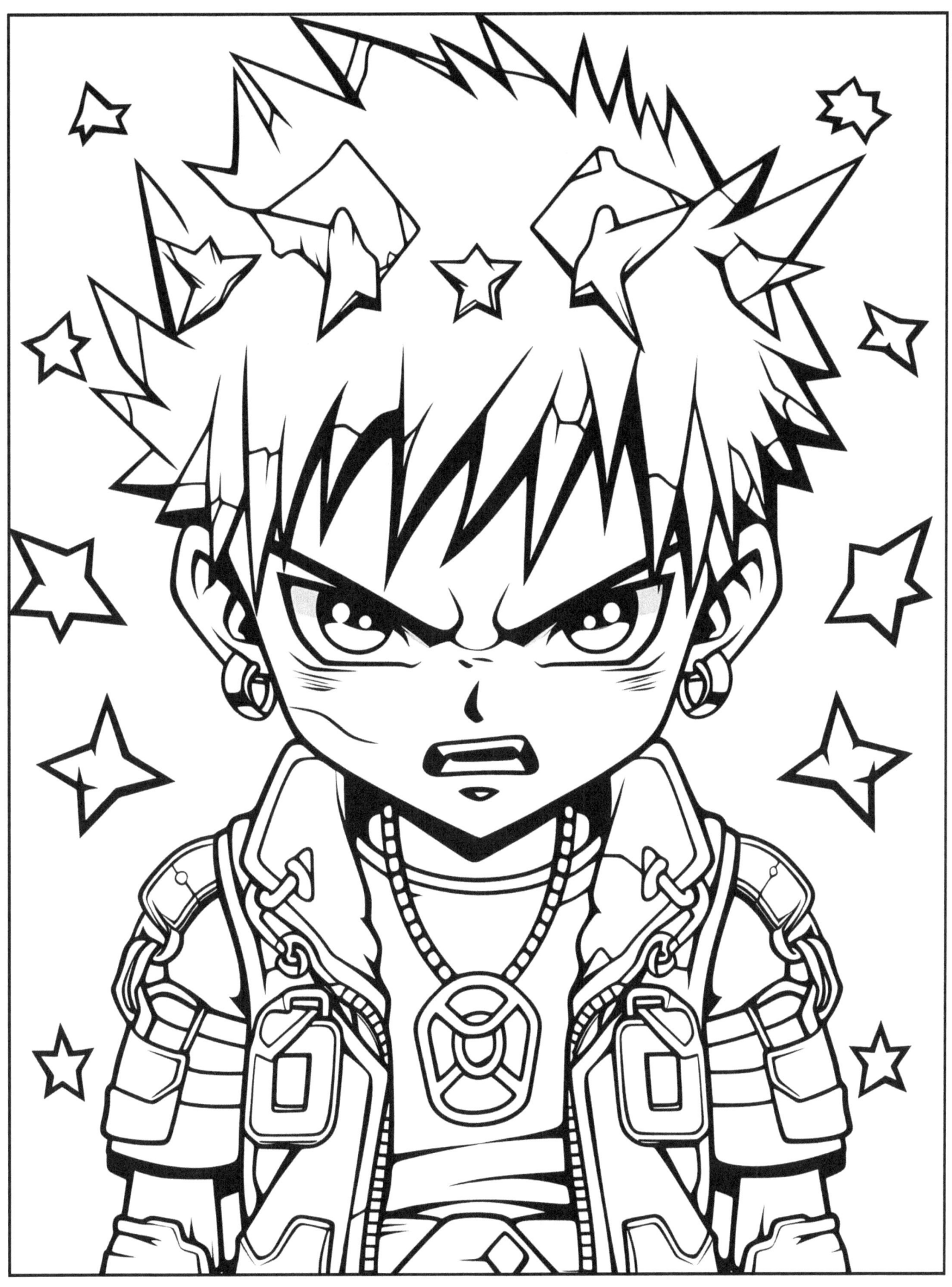

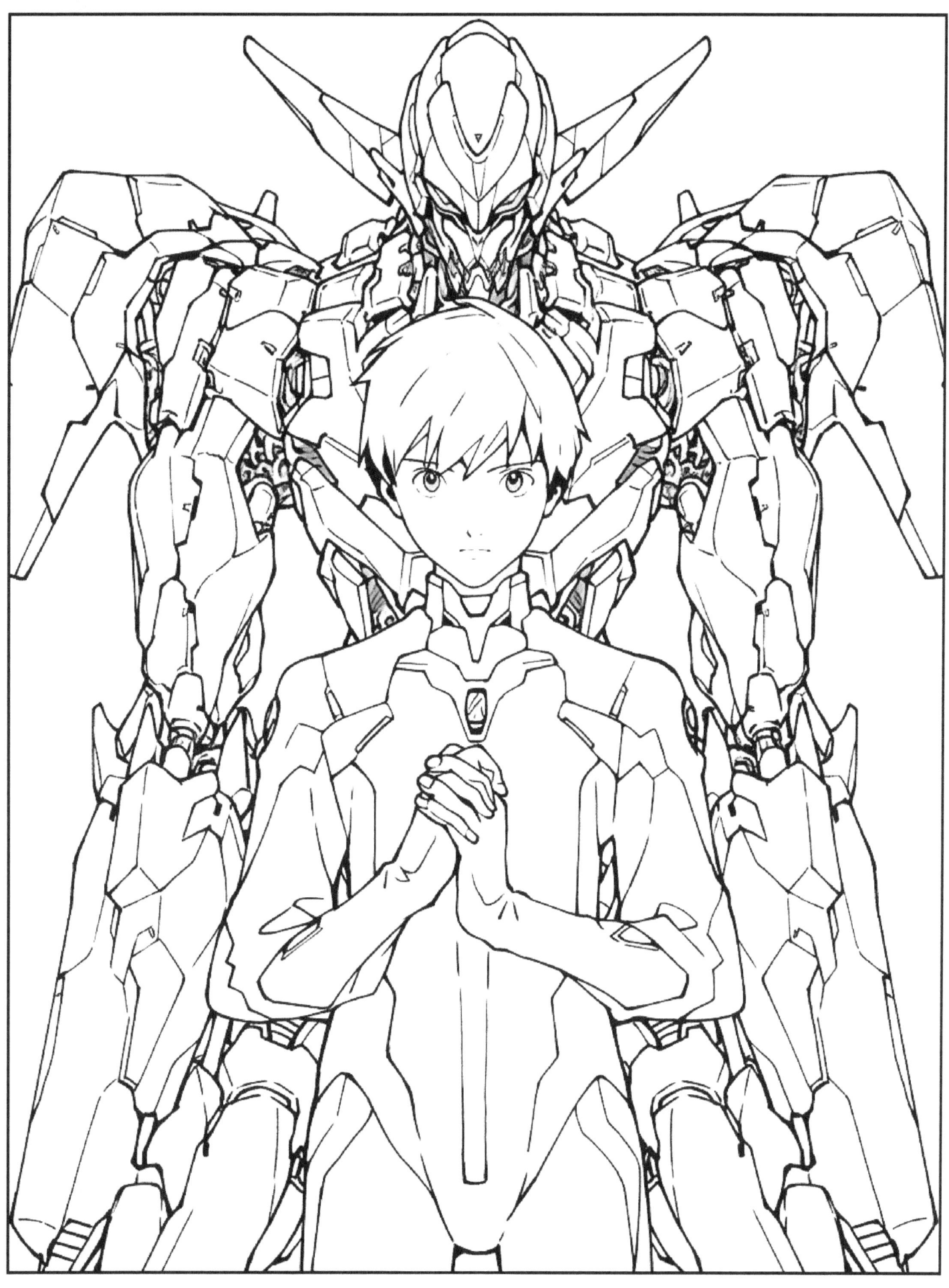